Murder & Mystery in New Mexico

Drawing By Peter Hurd

In memory of
Harvey Butler Fergusson
who believed in law and order

ERNA FERGUSSON

MURDER & MYSTERY IN NEW MEXICO

THE LIGHTNING TREE, SANTA FE, N.M. 87504

Library of Congress Catalog Card No. 91-60889

ISBN: 0-89016-098-8 (paperback)

ISBN: 0-89016-099-6 (cloth bound ltd. ed.)

The limited edition of this book celebrates
the 20th Anniversary of the New Mexico Book League
—an exemplary force in the writing, publishing and
promotion of books in the Southwest

Manufactured in the United States of America

First Lightning Tree Printing

The Lightning Tree—Jene Lyon, Publisher
Post Office Box 1837
Santa Fé, New Mexico
U. S. A.

Contents

1. The Vigilantes of Socorro — 15

2. The Ballad of Manuel B. — 33

3. Billy the Scapegoat — 49

4. The Mystery of the White Sands — 73

5. How Black Jack Lost His Head — 95

6. A Navajo Killing — 113

7. The Manby Mystery — 133

8. Woo Dak San and the Bird — 153

9. New Mexico Tries Its Own — 171

The Photographs — 197

New Mexico was annexed to the United States in 1846. All its inhabitants were then citizens of Mexico and were called Mexicans until about 1918 when Spanish-American was preferred. In this book Mexican is used wherever anything else would be anachronistic.

Foreword

Probably people are never so much themselves as when they are killing or being killed. Perhaps there is no better way to know a people than to understand why they kill. Not only the moment's hot compulsion but all the deep currents of thought and habit that made that killing at that time seem both right and necessary to the killer.

This is most true in New Mexico where within the memory of living men and women killing has come all the way from a manly and needful act to an intolerable offense. Good men, in all eras, have regard for the general good; bad men consider only their own selfish ends. But what seems good in one period may seem evil in another. Standards change as surely as times change.

This book is about all kinds of killers, evil and good. It also suggests some of the evil done by men who were not remembered as killers, but whose acts made killers of others.

These are true stories and hence have no neat solutions. Many of them remain official mysteries. Others, in which somebody was tried and found guilty, leave the speculative observer filled with questions. How did it happen that this, of all similar situations, resulted in the violence of murder? Why was this man and no other brought to trial? Or why was nobody tried? Who was really to blame?

1. The Vigilantes of Socorro

It was Christmas Eve, 1880. The little town of Socorro looked as peaceful as Bethlehem under a far, cold sky spangled with the sharp stars of a New Mexico night. At nine o'clock the flat-topped adobe town showed three glowing spots of light and activity. The Catholic Church of Our Lady of Succor, built by the Spaniards a couple of centuries ago. There the faithful had performed the drama of the nativity, placing a tiny doll in the arms of a statue of the Virgin. There the congregation spoke Spanish; dons and their families — men in black cloth and leather, ladies in long black cashmere shawls — and peons who kissed the hands of their betters.

To the east, on the plaza, another sort of light and sound flamed and roared above saloons and gambling houses crowded with men on holiday. Charley Utter, with long shining curls and a row of diamond studs in his white shirt, dealt faro at the Monarch saloon, and in the back room his Mormon wife, Minnie, and Maude, another daughter of Brigham Young, ran the stud poker table.

There, surely, was the setting for a wild western tale: wide open gambling, drunken men, wicked women. But it was the third spot of light — the little adobe Methodist chapel out under the stars — that was to see the night's tragedy. There the Reverend Mathieson preached of the Holy Birth; children's voices piped in carols, and children's eyes watched the gifts on the Christmas tree. The air was hot from the glowing sheet-iron stove, and aromatic from the Christmas greens.

Mr. A. M. Conklin, editor of the *Socorro Sun,* was moving quietly about, directing the program, keeping order. He noticed that three young Mexican men were behaving rudely. As editor, he knew who they were; though as a newcomer he may not have understood their sacrosanct status as hidalgos nor known how to deal with them. Their name was Baca: Antonio, son of the most important Mexican in the county, Antonio María Baca; and Antonio's two nephews, Onofre and Abrán. One of them sprawled with his feet on the seat before him. Mr. Conklin asked him politely to take them down. Most families of such prominence as the Bacas were Catholic; but Protestant missionaries had long been active in New Mexico and the Bacas often attended services in Reverend Mathieson's church. As a rule they were impeccably well behaved.

Passing again, Mr. Conklin noticed the same Baca boot uptilted on the seat. He spoke again, and this time he moved the boot. The third time, when he saw the same young man rudely lolling with his boot pressing the edge of a lady's pelisse, Mr. Conklin's chivalry overcame his Christian fortitude and he spoke sharply, pushing the foot aside.

"You are welcome here," he said, "if you behave . . . If not, young man, you will have to get out!"

He went on, unaware that he had insulted a Mexican hidalgo, member of a class accustomed to deference in all cases. To Mr. Conklin, a rude young man was a rude young man; he did not realize that his words had roused centuries of fierce Castilian pride. So he went on with his duties, distributing Christmas presents, snuffing candles that burned too low. Then the meeting ended and the congregation, laughing and chatting, drifted out of the stuffy church into the frosty air. As Mr. Conklin stepped through the door with his wife on his arm, one of the Bacas approached him.

"May I speak to you a moment?" The voice was low, the gesture friendly.

Mr. Conklin, unsuspecting, turned in response to a gentle hand on his right arm, as another man pulled Mrs. Conklin away from his left. Then, from a man standing by a horse in the darkness, came a vicious blaze of orange light, the crack of a shot. Mr. Conklin took one uncertain step, slumped, and crumpled quietly to the ground, shot through the heart. Mrs. Conklin screamed. The crowd pushed, turned, and hesitated, not knowing what to do. In that moment of indecision, three young men leapt to their horses and galloped away in the dark. Everyone had recognized them as Antonio Baca and his two nephews, Onofre and Abrán.

In no time the news reached the plaza. Men rushed out of saloons and gambling houses. A hundred times the tale was told. A gringo shot by a Mexican! A gentle, inoffensive man, assisting at a Christmas party, shot to death as he walked out of church with his wife on his arm!

"Damned greasers!" . . . "Just one thing they understand and that's a knife in the guts!" . . . "There's a way to handle them, all right."

A calmer voice, "Let the law take charge; call the sheriff." And a snort, "Sheriff, hell, Juan María García wouldn't lift a finger against a Baca; you'll see."

Everybody knew that becoming citizens of the United States had not altered the Mexicans' basic ways. The great families still ruled, lesser folk still felt themselves held in feudal thrall. The Baca family dominated Socorro as of old; inconceivable that one of their old-time retainers would take action against them. Sheriff Juan María García would act as a dependent of the Baca family; not as a free-born citizen and duly elected officer of the law. So men talked and swore, urging action but doing nothing. They were awaiting a leader.

Christmas morning, Colonel Ethan W. Eaton, home from his ranch for Christmas dinner, rode up to his house, gave his horse to a waiting lad, and strode through the *zaguán*. Even before greetings were over, his wife, his sons, and the servants had told him about the killing of Mr. Conklin.

Colonel Eaton, a tall, silent man, absolutely fearless, was never in any doubt as to what was right and wrong, and what should be done about it. A born leader of men. Without hesitation he sent a man to Sheriff García to demand the arrest of the murderers. Colonel Eaton probably did not expect the law to take its proper course, but he was proceeding correctly anyhow. Soon the messenger was back, grinning. Sheriff García could not be found. He was not at his office in the Court House, nor at his home, nor on the streets. Someone had said that he was hiding at the home of his deputy, who was also his son-in-law.

Colonel Eaton left his house, redolent now of the cooking Christmas turkey, and strode through the streets toward the deputy's house. As he went he was surrounded by other quiet men, all gringos. Colonel Eaton, commanding officer of the local militia, was the acknowledged leader. Of him one said: "The Colonel never talked much. All he ever had to do was say, 'C'mon, boys,' and jerk his head, and we'd do whatever he said." In this case they followed the Colonel to the deputy sheriff's house.

The men were shouting for García. Others muttered: "He'll never arrest a Baca!" . . . "He's been old Don Antonio María's man all his life!" . . . "Never should 'a been sheriff!" The most forthright had circled the house and from them came a shout: "Here they are!" Sheriff García and his deputy were leaving the house by a back way.

Colonel Eaton was the natural spokesman. "Sheriff García, we demand that you arrest the killers of Editor Conklin."

García gibbered with fear, "No! No!"

Without even a word from Eaton, the mob pushed him into their front rank and set out for Cuba, a mile or two south of Socorro, where the Bacas lived. García found himself going to the home of his *patrón* and relative, old Antonio María Baca, to arrest the Don's own son and two of his grandsons. Sheriff García was in an impossible position; in his tradition such a thing could not be!

At Cuba the men halted before the Baca home, a large adobe house with a long *portal*. In front of it ran a deep irrigating ditch, dry at that season. Colonel Eaton stationed most of his men in the ditch, while he advanced to the door, arm-in-arm with the trembling sheriff, and demanded the men who had killed Conklin.

"Not here," came a voice from within.

"Don't shoot, *Patrón*," yelled the Sheriff. "I'm here, and if you shoot you'll get me, sure!"

All this was in Spanish.

"Open, and let us see if they're not there."

"Not here," came a firm reply, "and we refuse to open."

"Bring on the dynamite," called someone in the ditch, and the Sheriff screamed, "Open the door or they'll blow up the house!"

So the heavy front door was opened, and the household filed out between two rows of watching men. Men, with their hands hanging to show they were unarmed; frightened children; Don Antonio María, walking with the dignity of a Roman senator and flashing scorn on the gringo mob which invaded his home; women, so muffled in fringed black shawls that it was impossible to tell the young from the old. Impossible even to tell which were women — until one demure lady made a quick leap onto a horse, a dropped shawl uncovering a man's haircut, skirts lifted shamelessly over a pair of active masculine legs. Antonio Baca!

They caught him, but Abrán walking ahead in the line got clean away, though they chased him for miles. He hid, no doubt, in some peon's hut and escaped finally across the line into Mexico. Of Onofre, they saw nothing.

The reluctant sheriff and his victorious posse conveyed Antonio to Socorro. Afraid to trust him to the jail, Colonel Eaton locked his prisoner in the Park Hotel which still stands at the southwest corner of the plaza. Many nervous women came there, fearing for panicky days an attack that never came.

Mr. Mathieson preached a dramatic funeral sermon over Mr. Conklin, and Mrs. Conklin, wild with grief and heartbroken, nevertheless decided to carry on the *Socorro Sun* with her husband's assistant editor to write the editorials.

Antonio Baca stayed in his locked room, guarded day and night. His relatives were allowed to bring him food and he fared well. His pretty sister, walking the streets with her duenna, amused herself by greeting gringo men with a melodious Spanish phrase: *"Mal a quien te parió!"* They found her charming. They would stamp and rattle their spurs so she would see them sweep off their big hats and bow. None of them could translate her rapid Spanish "Cursed be she that bore you!"

Antonio's guard had an uncomfortable time; the Mexican hidalgo was adept at looking scornful, when he condescended to speak he boasted that there would be no hanging for him.

One day the guard suddenly found himself looking into the barrel of a pistol in his prisoner's hand. It was a seven-shot gun, small enough to be concealed in a loaf of bread, but deadly. Antonio's eyes were hard as he pulled the trigger. But the guard was quick. His shot and the prisoner's sounded like one. Other men came running, but the first shot had killed Antonio, neatly drilling a hole in the side of his nose.

Now bitterness was intense; each side had a martyr. "Damned gringo!" offset "Damned greaser!" As these ugly ephithets showed, this was no usual killing of one man by another, a crime to be handled by officers who would see that justice was done. It caused an upsurge of deep hatreds, such as animate men who are ignorant of each other's ways. Within the memory of living men, New Mexico, a province of Mexico, had been occupied by United States troops. Most inhabitants had welcomed the bluecoats as protectors from marauding Indians; and assurance of such stability as the weak Mexican republic had not given them. The United States behaved most exemplarily; the new citizens were granted all rights and privileges, confirmed in their property rights, given the vote. But old habits, as always, were longer-lived than men; prejudices stronger than any laws.

The new citizens continued to live and to think as before: the *patrón,* the wealthy aristocrat, dominated and expected to; the peon, often a relative, but poor and illiterate, continued to do as the *patrón* said. This was the pattern of feudalism — far, indeed, from the democratic way of pioneers who had pushed westward all the way across the continent. They, in New Mexico, were for the first time faced with a settled population, a people they could not understand. Ignorant of any way of life not their own, these pioneers put down what they could not understand as wrong. Language, religion, customs — all were different, baffling, not right. To the Mexican, with his settled ways, formal manners, and "one true faith," the invader seemed a crude creature, bad-mannered, rough, often drunken, and a heretic. Both "gringo" and "greaser" had become fighting words, though gringo is best explained as a corruption of *Green Grow the Lilacs, Oh,* a song sung by US troops in the Mexican War; and greaser, as an extension of the word applied to hirelings who greased the pioneer's wagons. With a few honorable exceptions on both sides, this underlying pattern often made for ugly talk and vicious acts.

So the killing of Conklin by Baca set a match to tinder that lay forever ready. Mexicans rallied to the *patrón,* family honor and group loyalty were stronger than any concept of abstract justice. Gringos united to catch and punish the killers, legally or not. In the name of law enforcement, they were ready to proceed illegally.

22

So the Vigilantes of Socorro came about almost spontaneously. They called themselves the Committee of Safety. Colonel Eaton was their leader.

Two Bacas were still missing: Abrán, who got away in women's clothes; and Onofre, who had not been seen or heard of since the murder. Rewards were offered, and descriptions were posted everywhere. Inevitably, one was seen by James B. Gillette, a Texas Ranger stationed at Ysleta just south of El Paso. One day, Ranger Gillette saw two nice looking young men sitting on the porch with Judge José Baca, a relative of the Socorro family. On a chance he arrested them both and took them up to Socorro. One had no connection with the crime and was released. The other was Abrán, and he was jailed pending trial.

Onofre had not been caught, but Ranger Gillette was still on the job. A month later he heard of a suspicious young man working in a store at Saragosa, Mexico — five miles south of the border. Believing that a Ranger should always get his man, Ranger Gillette proceeded; but his proceedings were altogether irregular for an officer of the law. This is best quoted from Mr. Gillette's own account in his book, *Six Years As a Texas Ranger.*

"I knew," he wrote, "that I could not go into Saragosa, attempt to arrest a Mexican, stay there five minutes and live; yet I determined to take the law into my own hands. I took into my confidence just one man, George Lloyd . . . The next day Lloyd came to me and said, 'Sergeant, I will go anywhere in the world with you.'"

So two Texas Rangers invaded a friendly country without a shadow of legal right. Gillette writes as of a school boy lark.

"We reached Saragosa safely, and while Lloyd held my horse

in front of the store I entered and discovered Baca measuring some goods for an old Mexican woman. I stepped up to him, caught him by the collar, and with a drawn pistol ordered him to come with me. The customer promptly fainted and fell to the floor. Two other people ran from the building screaming at the top of their voices. Baca hesitated about going with me and in broken English asked me where he was to be taken. I informed him to El Paso del Norte. I shoved my pistol right into his head and told him to step lively. When we reached our horses I made Baca mount behind Lloyd. I then jumped into my saddle and . . . we left Saragosa on a dead run. Our sudden appearance in town and our more sudden leaving bewildered the people for a few minutes. They took in the situation quickly, however, and began ringing the old church bell rapidly, arousing the whole population . . . I saw men getting their horses together and knew that in a few minutes a posse would be following us. When we had gone almost two miles at top speed, I saw that Lloyd's horse was failing and we lost a little time changing Baca to my mount. We had yet two miles to go and through deep sand most of the way. I could see a cloud of dust and shortly a body of men hove in view. It was a tense moment . . . but we still had a long lead and our horses were running easily . . . As soon as they had drawn up within 600 yards they began firing on us . . . I believe they were trying to frighten rather than to wound us, as they were just as likely to hit Baca as either of us. We were at last at the Rio Grande, and while it was almost 100 yards wide, it was flat and shallow at the ford. I hit the water running and as we mounted the bank on good old Texas soil I felt like one who has made a homerun in a world series baseball game. Our pursuers halted at the river, so I pulled off my hat, waved to them and disappeared up the road."

So far, so good. But at the Rangers camp the arrival of two Rangers with rundown horses and a prisoner gathered such a crowd that Captain Baylor came over and asked pointed questions. Seeing that he could not put off his superior officer, Gillette decided to "fess up." "I told him that I had arrested Baca at Saragosa and kidnapped him out of Mexico. Captain Baylor's eyes at once bulged to twice their natural size. 'Sergeant, that is the most imprudent act you ever committed in your life. Don't you know it is a flagrant violation of the law and is sure to cause a breach of international comity that might cause the Governor of Texas to disband the whole of Company "A"? . . . it is a wonder to me that the Mexicans did not shoot you and Lloyd into doll rags.' "

Nevertheless, Captain Baylor permitted his imprudent men to proceed with their prisoner by horse to Rincon, the terminus of the Santa Fe Railroad at that time.

Gillette's account continues: "I wired the officers of Socorro from El Paso that I had captured Onofre Baca and was on my way to New Mexico with him. Baca's friends had also been informed of his arrest and lost no time in asking the Governor of New Mexico to have me bring the prisoner to Santa Fe as they feared mob violence at Socorro. When I reached San Marcial I was handed a telegram from the Governor, ordering me to bring Baca to Santa Fe and on no account to stop with him in Socorro. I did not reach Socorro until late at night. The minute the train stopped at that town it was boarded by twenty-five or thirty armed men. I showed them the Governor's telegram, but they declared Baca was wanted at Socorro and that was where he was going. I remonstrated and declared I was going on to Santa Fe with the prisoner. By this time a dozen armed men had gathered around me and declared, 'Not much will you take him to Santa Fe.' I was furious but I was practically under arrest and powerless to help myself. Baca and I were transferred from the train to a big bus that was in waiting. The jailer entered first, then Baca was seated next to him and I sat next the door with my Winchester in my hand. The driver was ordered to drive to the jail.

"I then informed the mob of the nature of Baca's arrest and told them that the hanging of the prisoner would place me in an awkward position. Then, too, the reward offered by the Territory of New Mexico was for the delivery of the murderer inside the jail doors of Socorro County. The leaders of the crowd consulted for a few minutes and then concluded I was right. They ordered me back into the bus, gave me my Winchester, and we all started for the jail. As soon as Baca had been placed in prison someone wrote me a receipt for the delivery of Baca inside the jail doors.

"The men took Baca to a nearby corral and hanged him to a big beam of the gate. The next morning Baca's relatives came to me at the hotel, with hats in their hands, and asked me for the keys with which to remove the shackles from the dead man's legs. As I handed them the keys I felt both mortified and ashamed."

This was not quite the end of Ranger Gillette's escapade, for the Baca family made representations to Washington and Captain Baylor was called to account for his men's flagrant violation of all law. "But," Ranger Gillette writes complacently, "Captain Baylor was a fluent writer," and one who would stand by his men to the bitter end. What he wrote to the Governor of Texas or the

Washington authorities is not recorded, but the affair was dropped and Ranger Gillette collected the reward and continued as a Texas Ranger in good standing.

Two Bacas were then accounted for. Abrán, awaiting trial, was let alone and his case came up at the fall term of court in '81. He was defended by R. E. M. Farland, and Moore and Shaw. The prosecuting attorney was Colonel J. Francisco Chaves, a dapper French-looking and very powerful gentleman of Spanish extraction. The jury was all Mexican. Baca pleaded not guilty. The trial lasted several days, during which the court room was filled with men, mostly members of the Safety Committee.

As Colonel Chaves closed the case for the prosecution he dropped into Spanish, a natural thing to do in addressing a jury whose native language was his own; but it was ill-advised.

"Gentlemen," he said, "remember, as you consider this case, that you are faced with a case of cold-blooded, unprovoked, inexcusable murder. I charge you to forget all considerations of family, friendship, or race, and to render your decision in accordance with the law and the facts. I charge you, gentlemen of the jury, do your duty at all costs."

Most of the new Safety Committee did not understand Spanish. What was this Mexican saying to his jury of Mexicans? He was of the class that had commanded their class for generations. The Safety Committee did not like the look of it.

The Judge made his charge. The jury retired. In a very short time they returned. The prisoner stood to hear their verdict. "Not guilty!" The Judge pronounced the prisoner free. Like a flash, Baca turned away from the court room full of angry gringos. One long step, a leg over the window sill, and he had dropped out of sight.

They say that he landed astride a horse held for him there, and in a moment was out of sight and away.

Colonel Chaves remained in the court room, and attention centered on him. A committee waited on him and escorted him to the depot. No passenger train was due for several hours, but a freight stood on the siding, ready to start. The committee had ropes. There were trees handy. They advised Colonel Chaves to leave on the freight train, and they urged him never to come back again.

"I'll leave," said Colonel Chaves, "and I'll come back whenever my business brings me."

So the tale of the Bacas ends, but the Safety Committee went on. To most citizens it was known as the Vigilantes, but the Mexicans, always realistic, called its members *Los Colgadores,* the Hangers. At first many of the best business and professional men were members, but soon Socorro's Safety Committee went the way of all extra-legal powers and grew lawless itself. Socorro, from being a peaceful hamlet surrounded by rich haciendas, had become a railroad town surrounded by rich mining country. Section crews who laid the tracks were the roughest sort of men; when gold was discovered in the Magdalena Mountains, mines and smelters contributed their quota of hard citizens; outlaws from the cattle country to the east found Socorro their handiest railroad town. When such men took over the Safety Committee, many others found it expedient to join.

One peaceful citizen admitted that he had joined when he was brought into a room full of men "hung all over with six-shooters." Asked about the oath of allegiance he had sworn to, he said: "I dunno. I didn't read it, I just wanted to sign it and get out of there." So the Safety Committee was recruited.

Once they captured a Mexican accused of rape, took him out at midnight, and put a rope around his neck. Asked if he had anything to say, the victim spoke with the fatalism of his people.

"It appears," he said in Spanish, "that it is the will of God and of the people that I should die. If my friends ask for me, say that I believe I have gone to a better world."

"Guilty or not guilty?" called someone.

Sam Meek, who was married to a Mexican woman and who spoke Spanish like his native tongue, said quickly: "He says he's guilty." So the rope was pulled, and the man died. The next day it was fully established that he was innocent.

Vigilantes, living until recently, admitted that some of their latest actions were hard to justify. Also they are hard to verify, as men who remember prefer not to talk and those who took part decline to be implicated. The gaudiest stories are on their way into myth and legend. Meanwhile, within two years of their founding as a private effort to establish public law and order, the Vigilantes had become an outlaw organization. But they were destined to stage one last spectacular hanging.

Joel Fowler was a slim, short, dark fellow who had as desperate a reputation as Billy the Kid, but without that boy's engaging qualities. He owned a big ranch where he employed many men. Some he paid off; some disappeared and were never heard of again. Men believed that Fowler often found it cheaper to kill than to pay. Some of his killings seemed justified to the ethics of his day; but often he went crazy-bad and killed for lust of killing. Such an affair was his last murder.

In '83 Fowler sold his ranch for fifty thousand dollars and came to town to celebrate. At last, Cale, a friend, tried to disarm him as he raged around the Grand Central Hotel. Fowler, wild, savage, drunken, turned on his friend with an open knife and slashed him viciously in the abdomen. A Texas cowboy rushed down the stairs into the midst of the row and caught the dying Cale as he fell.

It was all very confused, but Will Hardy, bank cashier, believed that the Texan, and not Fowler, killed Cale. The day after the killing that cowboy came into the bank with a knife he wanted to give away, a double-edged dirk about six inches long and with a handle shaped like a coiled snake. Hardy refused it, and the Texan gave it to Frank Vigil. Hardy was a cautious young man, and he did not offer this bit of evidence. Fowler should have been hanged anyhow, he thought.

Fowler was arrested and brought to trial for the killing of Cale. The Vigilantes sat in the court room, stern, unrelenting, watchful. Evidence was introduced to show that Cale died from a wound six inches deep, while Fowler was armed only with his pocket knife. Still he was found guilty, to the general approval. His attorney, Neill B. Field, asked for and got a continuance. That was enough for the Vigilantes. The law had had its chance.

There was little doubt what would happen next. Attorney Field, young and new to New Mexico, was appalled at the calmness men showed in assuming that a lynching was next in order. He decided to appeal to Socorro's better nature. So he mounted the plaza wall, a handsome man with reddish hair and mien somewhat portentous for one so young. He spoke of justice, of the law, of orderly processes, of many things that held no interest for Socorro. But his last words did. "If," he declaimed, "one hair of my client's head is touched, I shall leave Socorro forever." Years later one of the Vigilantes told the tale. "What else," he inquired, "could we do? We just had to hang Fowler after that!"

Then came the night that even the canny Will Hardy was to be a Vigilante. It was a cold night in January, 1884. Fowler was in jail. Everyone else, it seemed, was on the prowl.

Dr. Duncan, called out to see a patient, was stopped by a "Halt!" at a dark corner and advised to go home. The Doctor decided that his patient would do well enough until morning.

Will Hardy, laughing at the timid tenderfoot he was, remembers bumping into a Vigilante on a corner. Hoping he had not been recognized, he slid into a dance hall, grabbed a girl and danced for his very life. But he was followed and ordered out into the street. There the trembling young man was backed into a doorway in an adobe wall so thick that he could stand in the embrasure. Soon another young man was backed in beside him, Henry May. It was as black as the inside of your hat, but the two nervous youths could hear men moving about the jail across the street.

The jailer was summoned from the jail, overpowered and trussed up. Then they brought Fowler out, loaded with the chains which had tethered him to a stake in the dirt floor of his cell. Fowler was cursing, raging, threatening, offering bribes. Hardy says he heard no begging, though Fowler improved the opportunity to lay the blame for all his misdeeds on the dance hall girl he had married. He asked them to shoot him, or to let him jump from a wall with a rope around his neck. But Joel Fowler's captors thought he deserved the most ignominious death, and they jerked him off the ground. Hardy thinks that he was dead before that last pull, because in the struggle Fowler had been hit on the head.

Then a committee adjourned to a nearby room to decide the fate of Hardy and May. It was a small room, with only one door, two high barred windows, and it was jammed with about thirty armed and masked men. The question was whether to hang these two white-faced youngsters, jail them for future hanging, or admit them to membership in the lodge. Hardy was heartily in favor of membership. When May understood that the oath of allegiance promised mutual protection of all members, he demurred, all trembling as he was, on the ground that he hated Cock-eyed Fischer and didn't want to protect him.

Hardy punched him with an elbow. "Shut up, you fool," he whispered. "Promise anything until we get out of here."

So they promised and signed, and the Safety Committee was stronger by two members.

In the morning, Pete Simpson, the Sheriff, cut Fowler's body down. A coroner's jury found that he had come to his death at the hands of persons unknown. Mothers took their children to see Fowler's body as it lay in the court house, so they should understand the fate of bad men.

The Fowler hanging was the last appearance of the Safety Committee. The next year Charley Russell was elected sheriff, and everybody agreed that under him the law might be trusted to keep Socorro safe.

Law and order had reached the Rio Grande.

2. The Ballad of Manuel B.

Early on a hot August morning in 1883, Manuel B. Otero drew rein in front of a little cabin in the Manzano Mountains. He was on a serious mission, but he stopped to greet his old friend, Mrs. Louis Huning of Los Lunas, who had brought her children and a couple of servants into the mountains for a vacation. Years later Mrs. Huning told about that chat; later events stamped it deeply into her mind. She was fond of Manuel B., a handsome and charming young man; she loved to talk with him because he had studied at Heidelberg and could converse with her in her native tongue. The two families were closely linked because her three children were the age of Don Manuel's two; and his wife, the lovely Eloisa Luna, was a close friend. Mrs. Huning remembered the Luna-Otero wedding when the exquisite bride wore white satin with a coronet of pearls and orange blossoms and changed, in the afternoon, into a blue satin with Duchesse lace that the groom had brought from Brussels. So attired, she was ferried across the Rio Grande in a barge draped with red velvet for the great ball that night. Altogether, the joining of two of New Mexico's most prominent and wealthy families had been like a picture of old Spanish court life.

Don Manuel, standing now with hat in hand — for no gentleman would address a lady from his horse — gave Mrs. Huning news of Doña Eloisa, expecting her third child, and asked about her family. He did not mention the business that was taking him down to Antelope Springs. Perhaps Mrs. Huning had heard that there was some trouble with the Whitney's, a Boston family who disputed ownership of the ranch. But she did not remember that they spoke of it. She remembered only how handsome the twenty-three-year-old Manuel looked as he mounted his spirited horse, waved his hat to her, and rode off attended by two of his brothers-in-law and several peons.

Don Manuel was going to the Otero ranch house at Antelope Springs in response to a scribbled note from his *ranchero* there. "They have run me off. Come!" Not understanding what had happened, Don Manuel had come as quickly as he could. As he rode he could see the early mists lifting from the Manzano Range to the west. Eastward the mountains sloped steeply down to the long stretches of the Estancia Plains where myriads of antelope fed. It was rich grazing, thick with nourishing grama grass and showing an occasional spring, marked by cottonwoods, like La Estancia and Antelope Springs five miles to the north. This was now part of the Otero family's vast holdings, most of which were rich valley lands along the Rio Grande.

The Otero claim to these Estancia plains went back to 1819 when, as the Baca Grant, they had been awarded to Bartolomé Baca by the Alcalde, acting for the Governor of New Mexico and King of Spain. This is curious, for the Spanish king's armies had been defeated and the Republic of Mexico established in 1811. Apparently the Alcalde had not heard the news, for his report reads:

"I have placed him in possession, in the name of the King, whom may God preserve, and I took him by the hand and conducted him over the whole tract, shouting and plucking up grass and casting stones, in the name of the King . . . until I shed tears."

The tract was described as bounded by a line running from Cow Spring to the mountains, along the ridge to the Small Spring, to Flint Peak, and to Buffalo Spring. The vagueness of the survey was equaled by carelessness about the title. Naturally it was never confirmed by the King, and the Bacas neglected to clear their title under Mexican law. They used the land for years, grazing stock there under the old Spanish law providing that nobody might own grazing land outright, but that "pastures shall be common to all inhabitants thereof, present and to come."

Before the United States occupied New Mexico in 1846, Manuel Antonio Otero, father of Manuel B., bought half that Bartolomé Baca grant in Mexico for 500,000 pesos. His brother later bought the other half, bringing their holdings up to 1,232,000 acres. Both Oteros were unaware of the fact, which later impressed the United States courts, that the original Baca had never perfected his claim. They were dealing with Mexico, where records were not too well kept; letters were carried on mule or horseback; often it took months to get a reply; it is not surprising that the Alcalde had made a grant in the King's name after Mexico was a republic.

The Whitney's conflicting claim was based on a grant made by Governor Manuel Armijo of New Mexico to Antonio Sandoval in 1845. It consisted of about 300,000 acres of land, right out of the middle of the old Baca Grant, and was known as the Estancia Grant. At this time New Mexico was still a province of Mexico and Governor Armijo was acting for the government of that republic. The heirs of the Baca Grant seem to have made no protest. In time, Sandoval deeded the land to his nephew, Gervacio Nolan, and the heirs of Nolan sold to Joel P. Whitney, a Boston millionaire who placed his young brother James in charge of it.

It was a nice legal question, involving the laws of land ownership and usage of three countries: Spain, Mexico, and the United States. When the United States took over New Mexico from Mexico in 1846, the whole territory was filled with such conflicts. Under the treaty, the United States recognized all Spanish and Mexican grants, and gave patents to anyone who could prove ownership. In case of conflict, the United States recognized the prior claim as valid. In this case, Otero's claim, based on the uncontested Baca occupancy and use, was prior. Whitney contended that Baca had never perfected his title, that he claimed more than could be granted to one man under Spanish law, and that his heirs' failure to contest Governor Armijo's grant to Sandoval indicated that they did not consider their holdings permanent.

The Oteros could show that no record of the grant to Sandoval could be found in the Mexican archive. So to his claim of priority, Otero could add the contention that Sandoval's title was inchoate, never completed. As Sandoval obviously could not deed to Nolan what he did not own, Nolan's heirs could not make legal transfer to Whitney. Therefore, Otero's lawyers advised him, Whitney had no real right to the Estancia Grant. All this was in litigation in August, 1883. Why, then, was Manuel B. Otero riding over to meet Whitney at Estancia Springs? Because James G. Whitney was too impatient to wait on the slow processes of the law.

While his case against Otero was pending, Whitney had secured judgment against McAfee, one of the many squatters on the land he claimed. McAfee's attorney was preparing an appeal, but McAfee settled out of court with Whitney who agreed to pay for his cattle, his improvements at Antelope Springs and a small bonus to boot. Whitney then undertook to treat Otero as another squatter. But here he had a man of different caliber. Manuel B. was no small squatter to be removed with a word and a few dollars. To him, Whitney was the squatter who had moved in on land to which he had no right or title. Of a proud governing group, young Otero was fiery by nature, a fearless fighter, a good shot, and a man not at all averse to meeting his enemy face to face. So here he was, riding down the slope toward Estancia Springs.

A mile or two from that oasis, they met Longino Bustamente, herding a few hundred wethers. Doffing his hat, Longino spoke earnestly: *"Patrón,* don't go. Whitney is there with seven men. For days they have been watching for you through their long glasses. They say that if you come they will kill you." It was not the way to deter Manuel B. Otero. He even refused Bustamente's offer to go along. "No," he said, "I don't want them to think I am afraid. We'll go on."

By then the sun had driven the mists away and the yellow-green plain was a-shimmer with heat. The ranch house was a one-room adobe shaded by a couple of cottonwoods. Several cowboys lolled in the shade or squatted on their heels. To their keen eyes, Manuel B. and his friends, riding briskly up, did not look as though they had come to vacate.

Manuel B. tossed his reins to a peon and walked up to the house. He was slim and hard, straight and quick, with the blue eyes and red-blond hair of his family. Dr. Henríquez and Carlos Armijo were close behind him. The peons waited under the trees. Inside, Whitney and his brother-in-law, Alexander Fernández, and Arthur Bailache were sitting on the unmade bunks where they had slept. Whitney leapt to his feet as Otero appeared in the doorway with his two hands on the doorjamb.

"This is my house," said Otero, "by what authority are you here?"

"I've got a writ of possession up at Antelope Springs," said Whitney, insolently. "You might send one of your men to get it."

Otero's men were not running errands for Whitney.

"I'll not leave," said Don Manuel levelly, "until I see your authority."

Whitney whipped out his pistol. "This," said he, "is my authority."

Later he testified that he pulled his gun when he saw that Dr. Henríquez had him covered. Both shot. Fernández, on the bunk, was killed instantly and rolled under the bed. Otero, near the door, got a ball in the neck. He shot. Armijo, who had no gun, ran. Whitney fell, wounded in the jaw and in one hand. Otero staggered out the door, his pistol in one hand, the other clutching his neck. Henríquez was wounded in one hand, but he remained standing, covering Whitney and Bailache, both on the floor. Within as many

38

seconds ten shots had been fired. The small room was like a shambles, spattered with blood, stifling with smoke, and horrible with the groans of the wounded men.

"Give up now? Do you surrender?" yelled Henríquez.

Whitney mumbled weakly, "Tell my men to surrender."

The men outside, crowding against doors and windows, saw Otero stagger out, a smoking revolver in his hand, blood spurting from the wound in his neck. Longino Bustamente, who had followed after all, picked up Otero's gun as it fell and cried: "I'll kill the assassin, I'll kill him!" But Dr. Henríquez, his arm around Manuel, commanded sharply, "No more shooting. Help me here!"

Bailache emerged then, white and distraught, and set off at a run for the mountains. He ran as far as Chilili, some twenty miles, and there got a buggy to take him to Albuquerque where he told the first tale. Carlos Armijo also got a good start, running south. At La Estancia, so they say, he tipped his hat politely to a post and wished it a very good day, in the name of God.

Indoors, Dr. Henríquez, all physician now, had taken command. Ordering the men to put up their guns, he had got Otero onto a cot and was trying to stanch the bleeding from the carotid artery. At the same time, over his shoulder, he was directing Whitney's men in his care and sending a messenger to Antelope Springs.

Within a couple of hours the house was surrounded by half a hundred angry men from all the hamlets from Punta de Agua to Chilili. One of them, now more than eighty, says that when he got there Fernández' body lay on a table. Whitney was groaning on one of the bunks, and Otero lay on a cot with Dr. Henríquez beside him.

"I'd have shot Whitney myself," the old man shouted, still angry fifty years later. "I'd have killed the assassin myself if the doctor hadn't stopped me!"

During the afternoon, both Whitney and Otero dictated statements. Otero signed his, but Whitney was so weak that he could only make his mark. Otero told his men that he was not going to die, that he felt well, and he asked for whiskey. In his statement he said that he did not know whose shots had taken effect. Whitney said also that he did not know who had shot him, but he thought it likely that Otero and Fernández had shot each other.

Ed Haines, Whitney's nephew, had been galloping back and forth from Antelope Springs all day. About four in the afternoon he drove a wagon up to a back window, and they slid the dead Fernández and the wounded Whitney onto it, mattresses and all. Haines stated in a written version that he thought his uncle was in grave danger from Otero's men, and late that night took him on to Santa Fe.

Otero was weakening rapidly. The priest from Manzano had not come. They laid a mattress in a covered wagon, Dr. Henríquez made his patient as comfortable as he could, and they started on the long slow road to Los Lunas. Riders went ahead to bear the sad news to Doña Eloisa, assuring her that her husband was living. But the hundreds accompanying that sad cortege knew that their favorite Manuelito was going to die. At sunset he was gone. When his wife's brothers met them, with more hundreds of sorrowing friends and retainers, they could only proceed as a funeral procession. Doña Eloisa was a widow left with her two children, Adelina and Eduardo, and the third unborn whom she would call Manuel B.

The funeral brought relatives and friends from all parts of the territory, and it inspired obituaries in the flowery style of the period: "His spirit took its flight to the hands that gave it . . . and entered the bourne whence no traveller returns . . . we can only drop the sorrowing tear of friendship on the grave that holds all there is left save memory of Manuel B. Otero."

The editor of the *Albuquerque Morning Journal* undoubtedly expressed the general feeling in New Mexico: "Manuel B. Otero, the first victim of the bloody business, was a Mexican, an intelligent, educated gentleman, and . . . he was doing just what any American citizen would be expected to do under like circumstances — he was insisting upon his right to his home, and to property to which he had always held possession, and to which he had reason to believe his title was good."

The use of the word *Mexican* in a eulogistic obituary attracts attention now, but was customary then. The Oteros were Mexicans only in that New Mexico was part of the Republic of Mexico from 1811 until 1846. Before that they, like all the inhabitants of its vast empire, were colonials of Spain. But the Oteros had been New Mexicans since 1786 when Don Pedro brought his wife and small son, Vicente, from Spain to Santa Fe. The lady is said to have suffered from tuberculosis; seemingly New Mexico's climate was even then a lure. A year later Don Pedro acquired land in the lush Rio Grande Valley and named his new lands La Valencia in honor of his home in Spain.

The killing of Manuel B., scion of this proud line, naturally spread sorrow and dismay throughout the population of Valencia County. Many tributes appeared in the traditional form of verses to be sung. Casimiro Lujan, a famous minstrel of Torreon, composed a ballad and Doña Eloisa, in her widow's weeds, invited him to Los Lunas to sing it to her:

> "En el de 1883 desgraciado
> (In the unhappy year of 1883)
>
> Se vió Manuelito Otero
> (Little Manuel Otero was seen)
>
> En su sangre revolcado.
> (Weltering in his gore.)"

The chorus, rendered in a nasal minor, is repeated after each of the eleven verses, making the whole quite a test of endurance:

> "Indita de Manuel B.
> (The ballad of Manuel B.)
>
> Residente en la Constancia
> (Who resided in Las Constancia,)
>
> Por defender su nación
> (And who, for defending his lands,)
>
> Sufriste muerte sin causa.
> (Suffered death without justification.)"

The verses relate the details of the shooting of Manuel B. by an infamous one; his farewell to his lovely wife, Eloisa; names his mother and brothers; and ends:

> "Ante Dios pongo me queja
> (Before God I place my plaint,)
>
> Y al supremo tribunal
> (And to the supreme tribunal;)
>
> Que se ha de andar mi querella
> (My case must be stated at last)
>
> En una corte marcial
> (In the highest court —)
>
> Que mi muerte fué sin causa
> (That my death was unnecessary)
>
> Y me derecho legal.
> (And my cause was just.)"

Another ballad, composed by Plácido Romero of Peralta, reflects hatred of the foreigner who had killed the neighbor and friend. It describes the killer as a coward, a Texas robber, and a murderer whom devils await in hell which is the place *(la estancia)* for him. The killer was well known to be a Bostonian; the poet used the word *Texan* epithetically, not geographically — for the worst you could call a man was a Texan.

Back in Boston they saw it differently. The *Albuquerque Morning Journal* quoted one account: "Certain gentlemen from the East had purchased a valuable ranch; their title to the same was sustained by the Supreme Court of the Territory; but when they went to take possession of their property, they were met by an armed band of Mexicans who had squatted on the premises and refused to obey the order of ejectment, and the result was the murdering of two or three men."

If the Whitneys, reading the eastern press, had counted on popular sympathy, even among citizens not Spanish, they were in for a surprise. Even as James Whitney lay ill in St. Vincent's Hospital in Santa Fe, he was served with a warrant for the murder of Manuel B. Otero. A twenty thousand dollar bond was demanded.

St. Vincent's was then directed by Sister Blandina Segale, whose book *At the End of the Santa Fe Trail* reflects an intrepid spirit exalted by a pure faith. When James Whitney was brought in, Sister Blandina wrote, "I asked Sister María Teresa if she were ready to make an unusual sacrifice. She asked if it concerned her brother Manuel. I answered 'Yes . . . Are you willing to visit him as a patient and during your visit make yourself known and say "I forgive?" '

"Her response was slow, but deliberate.

" 'I will visit him as a patient and will say: "I forgive you as I hope to be forgiven, I am Manuel Otero's sister." ' "

Sister Blandina closes the episode by saying, "that same night the patient was spirited out of the hospital." He was indeed. Under the noses of hospital attendants, county and territorial officers, James Whitney, still a stretcher patient, was carried out of the hospital, put aboard the private car in which his brother had sped to his side, and started to California by way of Denver.

Governor Sheldon at once wired young Miguel Otero, a cousin of the dead Manuel, to get the sheriff of San Miguel County, stop the train and bring the prisoner back. "Gillie," who was destined to be one of New Mexico's most brilliant and picturesque governors, was then twenty-four years old, five feet five inches tall, afraid of nothing, loving a ruction, and delighted with the assignment. He and the sheriff flagged the train at Sulzbacher station, got aboard and demanded the prisoner. Joel P. Whitney protested. Gillie shoved his gun into the plutocrat's stomach, showed his deputy's badge, and went on in. The car was dropped from the train, to be picked up an hour later by a southbound train. James Whitney was headed at last for Los Lunas.

At Lamy, the party was joined by Tranquilino Luna, Manuel B.'s brother-in-law and Deputy Sheriff of Valencia County, and the sheriff of Santa Fe County who agreed to permit the Whitneys to send telegrams. As a result the train was boarded in Albuquerque by the Whitney's attorneys, who brought a writ of habeas corpus and the District Judge. Judge Bell, holding court in the private car, heard Whitney's attorneys plead that their client's life would be in danger in Los Lunas where an angry mob was gathering. Doctors testified that the prisoner's condition required rest and quiet. Joel P. Whitney, who had put up bond, said he thought he was free to take his brother away. The Judge found the papers in order and permitted the Whitneys to depart for California, leaving a storm of conflicting stories.

Joel P. Whitney was a wealthy man with money invested in the territory, and more to invest. One newspaper lauded him as a great man and mentioned naively that he was pleased with the treatment accorded him. Others hinted broadly that only the Whitney millions had held the train for so irregular a performance as a session of court in a private car.

That the Whitneys used money is open to question. That they used acumen cannot be doubted. They had employed Colonel José Francisco Chaves of Peralta as their attorney. Colonel Chaves, who had served in the American army and as delegate to Congress from New Mexico, was a member of a family quite as important and powerful as the Oteros, and their natural rival for the control of Valencia County.

One observer of these doings, asked if Whitney would have been in danger in Los Lunas, answered: "Oh, no, not when he got *el Coronel* Chaves for his lawyer. *El Coronel,* you see, had the district judge by the ear."

The next April, Whitney appeared in court in Los Lunas quite safely. Pleading that he could not get a fair trial in a county composed mostly of friends, relatives, and retainers of the Otero and Luna families, his attorneys got a change of venue. The trial was held on April 29, 1884 in Colfax County, far from the scene of the shooting.

Most of the territorial papers reported the trial with suspicious lack of detail. Only a few editorials show that feeling was running high. It was suggested that Whitney was to be "persecuted as well as prosecuted." Judge Axtell, who was to hear the case, was presented with a petition, "numerously signed by Mexican residents," calling his attention to the makeup of the jury. Colonel Chaves and his associates, three prominent gringo lawyers, had succeeded in getting a jury which did not include one Spanish name: something unlikely to happen in New Mexico without design. It was a cowboy jury, and all the proceedings were in English.

The *Las Vegas Optic* said: "They say that Whitney's jury was the very best body of men that ever sat in the jury box in this territory. That's what Judge Axtell thinks, and what Whitney thinks. The people have not expressed themselves yet."

Mrs. Whitney was there: an effective picture in deep mourning for her brother, Alexander Fernández, and with her children beside her.

Dr. Henríquez was the strongest witness for the prosecution, according to John Taylor of Springer, the only man living in 1935 who had served as juror in that trial.

Mr. Taylor said: "I don't think a man on the jury was prejudiced because Otero was a Mexican. We liked Whitney's looks and his gameness on the stand. Up to the testimony of that doctor from Las Vegas, it looked pretty bad for Whitney. But when Dr. Mills walked into the court he made Henríquez look pretty flat."

Dr. Mills' testimony, as told fifty years later, does not seem very devastating. He deposed that he had met Dr. Henríquez on his way to join Manuel B. at Estancia. The Doctor was armed, it seems, and his conversation indicated that he anticipated a fight. In New Mexico in those days most men went armed. "Not," as one old Mexican phrased it, "that we expected a fight, but we was goin' to be ready if they was one."

Still, it was enough for the jury. They stayed out, Mr. Taylor remembered, only long enough for a smoke, and then brought in a verdict of "Not Guilty." Mr. Whitney, who had not spoken to them before, shook hands and thanked them all.

The *Las Vegas Optic,* reporting the verdict, said: "Whitney is a man about thirty-one years of age, is about five feet six inches tall, has dark hair and mustache, and is withal a very promising looking fellow. With his good looking face and PLENTY of money, and the judge to instruct for him, NO WONDER he was discharged."

The editor adds, bitterly, the old western classic: "A man who kills another in New Mexico has a much better show than if he stole a cow."

The case of the land grant, detached from the personal tragedies it had evoked, rocked along for years in the Court of New Mexico Land Claims, founded to unravel the multitude of such disputes, and finally reached the Supreme Court of the United States. The final decision, in 1898, found both parties right as to the faultiness of the other's claim. Baca, according to the decree, had never completed his claim and never owned his grant. Sandoval, equally, had never owned his. So both grants were declared public domain and thrown open to settlement. Now the fine grassy stretches of the Estancia Valley are checkered with fences around forlorn little houses where perennially hopeful farmers are trying to prove that beans can be raised without water.

The irony of the tragedy was that though each man believed he was right, both were in fact wrong. It was all for nothing that two high-spirited and impetuous young men had shot each other in that blood-spattered room by the big Estancia Spring.

3. Billy the Scapegoat

Women liked Billy the Kid. And what a variety of women! Not dance hall sirens and crack-shot wild women; or if they did we have not their reports. Those we know about or can quote are a nun, a missionary's wife, a cultivated lady, a motherly Irish lady who saw him in jail; inarticulate emigrant women; simple peasant women who hid him, fed him, lied for him; young women who danced with him and loved him; the Navajo serving woman who found him dead and wailed "They have killed my little boy!"

How could it be that this gambler, cattle-thief, killer and desperado won the friendship of women who most depended upon the protection of law and a settled way of life? Was it his beauty? He was slim, erect, quick and graceful in his movements and a

fine dancer. His face was given an odd permanent grin by two buck
teeth that lifted the upper lip; far from beautiful but perhaps
engaging. His manner was what most wins women: easy deference
and considerate helpfulness. A natural gentlemen one called him.

Perhaps these extraneous charms drew women. But perhaps
good women knew instinctively what modern psychiatry has taught
us; that a person must be judged not by abstract ideas of right and
wrong, but by how he comports himself in the situation as he sees
it. Forced beyond the pale when he was twelve, Billy the Kid acted
the man consistently until he was killed when he was twenty-one.
One must remember too that seventy years ago in New Mexico, all
men went armed; a man was expected to look out for himself
instead of yelling for the police or developing a neurosis. A man
was judged either brave or a coward. Billy was always brave. Some
men thought Pat Garrett, who killed him, was a coward because
he shot an unarmed man in the dark. Garrett was an officer of the
law, Billy was wanted for murder. But those things, too, changed.
In the Lincoln County War, which involved a hundred civilians
and a troop of colored cavalry, the men opposing the sheriff
certainly showed themselves most admirable even by modern
standards. By the standards of either then or now, Lt. Colonel
N. A. M. Dudley, of the US Army behaved in a questionable
manner, though the Army gave him a complete whitewash later.
Billy's side lost, and he became an outlaw, charged with the murder
of the sheriff. His many friends, both men and women, thought
he was unjustly dealt with then; that he might have become a useful
citizen instead of a hunted creature, doomed to a criminal's death.

The first woman in Billy's life was his mother. Certainly he
loved her, and when his father died, young William Bonney had

the unsettling experience of seeing her remarry. His step-father, Antrim, was unkind to Billy, or the child thought so. The Bonneys had drifted west from New York where Billy was born in 1859. In Kansas the father died and in Colorado the widow married Antrim. In Santa Fe, Billy's delicate hands first showed their deftness; by the time he was eight the boy was a skillful monte dealer. Saloons and gambling houses were on his regular routes. Mrs. Antrim did her best for her son. In Silver City, where there were no public schools, she sent him to a private teacher though she was taking in boarders to support the family. One of the boarders was Ash Upson, known throughout the territory as a newspaper man and a trustworthy observer. He reported that Billy did well in school, learning easily. He endeared himself to people with his soft and courteous ways, especially with old people, children, and all women. But, even then, little Billy Bonney had a vicious temper and a nature that never forgot a friend nor forgave an enemy. All this came out in his first lawless act.

He overheard a man make an insulting remark about his mother on the street. Billy, aged twelve, jumped right at the man, twice his size, landed one blow and was picking up a rock when Ed Moulton, a prominent citizen, knocked out the bully and won Billy's undying friendship. So it was only natural that Billy, seeing Moulton about to be bested in a fight some time later, should dash into the fray. With his open pocket-knife the boy slashed one of Moulton's assailants who fell bleeding. The man did not die, but Billy thought he had killed him and he ran away.

William H. Bonney, alone and afoot with no money, had already demonstrated that he had courage, resourcefulness, and was not to be monkeyed with. Also that he could count on friends.

Jesse Evans, a Texas lad not much older, joined him and together they made their way into Arizona. Afoot, they did the obvious thing; "took" horses from some Apaches. As the Apaches had doubtless stolen the horses, Billy did as he was always to do; make his own decision as to who needed killing, and killed. His judgment would have been sustained by most of his contemporaries to whom the only good Indian was a dead Indian. They counted Billy's final total as "not including Indians."

Soon the boys parted, still the best of friends, and Billy made his way into Mexico where his easy Spanish and charming ways were sure to make him a success. His other gifts helped; he could outdeal almost anybody at monte, he was consistently lucky, and the hands that were so deft with cards were much quicker than the eye on the draw. It is rumored, but not proved, that Billy killed a couple of men in Mexico. Certainly he was becoming a phenomenal shot; he explained that when he drew he said to himself: "Point at what you want to hit," and pulled the trigger with his middle finger.

Back in New Mexico, Billy found that Jesse Evans had joined up with three men who were headed for the Pecos Valley: Billy Morton and Frank Baker who figured in Billy's story again, and Jim McDaniels who first called him the Kid. Billy the Kid he was from then on.

The Kid was not ready to head east. He had still to get a friend out of jail — Melquiades Segura, who had befriended him in Chihuahua. On a fine gray horse he rode eighty miles between six in the evening and midnight, bluffed the jailer, and got Segura free.

During these years it is difficult to follow Billy's career. Living the life of an outlaw, the Kid apparently always did what seemed to him right as well as expedient. He was loyal to his friends, took revenge on his enemies, looked out for himself, and got along all right. This made him a light-hearted youth, reveling in riding, shooting, cattle stealing. He relaxed at the dances where he was welcome. He loved to sing with cowboys. He was an addition to any party, even among the most correct people, for he had gentle manners and was never coarse nor profane. By this time, at seventeen, Billy had his growth of five feet seven inches, a light brown beard was beginning to show, his hair was waving, his blue eyes bright, his voice pleasant. Only when he was crossed did the protruding teeth look more like fangs than a grin, and the deep blue eyes blaze balefully down a gun barrel.

Incidents dealing with Billy the Kid are thick as scattered grain in the chickenyard, and as hard to arrange in any order. They reflect many points of view, but add up to a figure easy to understand against the background of his time and place.

Once he and Jesse Evans were entertained in an emigrant camp where the three men, obvious tenderfeet and quite unfit to look out for their women and several children, took a patronizing tone with the two callow youths. The youths, riding on ahead, came upon Apache tracks. The savages must be stalking the emigrants. In unhesitating agreement, Jesse and Billy wheeled about, cut over a saddle in the range, forced their horses to the point of collapse, and got to the camp just as the Indians attacked. The boys gave the warwhoop Billy was to make his own, and dashed to the rescue. It was a rescue, for though one of the men was killed, the women and children were saved, the Apaches driven off, and the wagons could proceed. These women never said what they thought of Billy the Kid. Nor did they need to.

Another incident suggesting knight-errantry has been told by Sister Blandina Segale, who never waited passively to be rescued. She tells, in her engaging book, *At the End of the Santa Fe Trail,* how she cared for one of the Kid's gang in Trinidad. He was wounded, alone, and with a tigerish gleam in his eyes, but he appreciated Sister Blandina's daily visits. One day he told the nun that the Kid was in town on purpose to kill Trinidad's four physicians who had refused to remove a bullet from his thigh.

As they talked, the Kid entered, swept off his big hat and scraped a polite foot. The nun noted that he "has steel-blue eyes, peach complexion, is young, one would take him to be seventeen — innocent-looking, save for the corners of his eyes which tell of a set purpose, good or bad." Billy incautiously offered to do for the nun anything she asked. At once she asked him to spare the doctors; she never told those worthies what had saved their lives.

Sister Blandina saw Billy once again — in circumstances that proved he never forgot a friend. In April, '78, Archbishop Lamy sent her to accompany the family of Adolph Staab as far as the railroad terminus near Trinidad. The party traveled with a train of freight wagons; Mrs. Staab and her two children in one carriage with Sisters Blandina and Augustine, Mr. Staab and two gentlemen in another. Every driver was a dead shot. The journey was uneventful.

On June 9, having seen Mrs. Staab and her children safely on the train, Mr. Staab and Dr. Symington debated the wisdom of starting back to Santa Fe. Billy the Kid was reported to be in the neighborhood and attacking all conveyances. But the nuns were serenely willing, the men had confidence in their fast team and in their own marksmanship. So they started, making Sweet Water for the night without incident. There the men cleaned, oiled, and loaded their guns, while the nuns said their beads. Considerably to their escorts' annoyance they persisted in performing this religious duty while walking up and down outdoors. But Sister Blandina, looking so meek, always had her way, so the men gave up and bade the nuns good night with "Do not be alarmed if you hear firing in the night; we shall protect you." Needless to say, the nuns slept as untroubled as usual.

The next day, the excellent span of horses, with its good Negro driver, sped spankingly along over the rolling green hills. The gentlemen were nervous, the driver shaking with fear. Soon he reported a horseman following, nearing, almost on them. Sister Blandina recognized him as he drew near. Billy the Kid! She tipped her bonnet back to give him a clear view of her face. "Our eyes met; he raised his large-brimmed hat with a wave and a bow, looked his recognition, fairly flew a distance of about three rods, and then stopped to give us some of his wonderful antics of bronco maneuvers."

She added: "I wondered if they did not connect . . . my persisting in saying our beads on the plains where all knew the members of the gang could see us with field glasses; if the connection could not be made, I had no intention of saying two and two are four, hence I kept silent."

We pick up the consecutive tale in 1877 when the Kid finally drifted into Lincoln County where there were jobs to be had. As he jogged along through the Guadalupe Mountains or detoured for a brush with Apaches, Billy the Kid was riding into the Lincoln County War with which his name would be forever linked and into a situation exactly suited to his talents.

That there was no law west of the Pecos was only too true. Even where legal forms had been set up, a man who was a law-abiding citizen when his party was in power, might find himself a hunted outlaw when it was not. The lawlessness natural to the frontier was, in New Mexico, being used by clever men to dominate both politics and business and to make one serve the other. Lincoln County was the perfect setting for such endeavor. Two hundred square miles of rich grazing land where frontiersmen roamed as free as men have never been since, and in the valleys Mexican hamlets and peaceful farms. Here were gunmen for hire, land for the taking, and owners who understood neither the language nor the customs of the newcomers.

In those free and easy days, when the cow country stretched from the Rio Grande to Canada without a fence, there was enough for all, and a newcomer had only to go out with rope and running iron, brand a few mavericks and start a herd. A cattle baron who had got his start that way would not demean himself by haggling over a calf. But times were changing. As the US Army established posts against the Indians, they offered a steady market for beef as well as hay and grain. Branding mavericks developed naturally into altering brands or killing on the range, hiding the hides, and selling the beef. Some Army officers and some Indian agents were not above buying stolen or tainted meat from a friend. John Chisum, "Cattle King of New Mexico," suspected that his "long rail" brand might be too easily altered. So he developed a cut on a calf's ear that resulted in his famous "jingle-bob."

Chisum's principal rivals were Fritz and Murphy who owned the biggest store in Lincoln Plaza on the Rio Bonita, and had friends in Fort Stanton and in Santa Fe. Colonel Emil Fritz was a German who had retired from the US Army. Lawrence G. Murphy had been trained for the priesthood. He was a jovial Irishman who often rode over to Fort Stanton for long nights of poker and whisky with the officers who bought supplies. The Fritz and Murphy firm soon had a monopoly on contracts for hay and grain as well as for beef. Their friends in Santa Fe were the men who, as the "Santa Fe Ring," were said to influence governors, intimidate judges, and have a long reach into county affairs. Law, in the sense of abstract justice and incorruptible courts, had not arrived. Men felt obliged to defend their interests, if need be, with their guns.

In 1875 one Alexander A. McSween appeared in Lincoln, bringing his young wife west in an oxcart. They stopped at the only two-storied house, the Fritz-Murphy store, and were promptly accepted as friends and associates. Mr. McSween, a lawyer from Pennsylvania, was regularly retained by the firm, and Mrs. McSween, well-born, sprightly, and charming, soon made her home one of those centers of culture so surprising to newcomers to the frontier. Alexander, eager to contribute to the culture of his new home, requested the missionary board in Philadelphia to send a minister for Lincoln. Scottish and Presbyterian, perhaps he held himself a bit self-righteously aloof from the convivial way of doing business between merchants and officers; soon he got in altogether wrong with Murphy by refusing a case he considered unjust. But he was prospering anyhow.

John H. Tunstall, a young Englishman with money to invest, had come into Lincoln County, bought land on the Rio Feliz, stocked it with cattle, and built a fine big adobe store in Lincoln. McSween became his manager, lawyer, and finally partner. Those two were as sure to be friends as both were sure to be uncongenial with Murphy and his new partner, James J. Dolan. Uncongeniality soon developed into enmity that split the county, as McSween and Tunstall became close friends and frequent visitors of John Chisum at his ranch down on the Pecos. "Honest John" took no active part, but he was the overpowering rival of the Murphy-Dolan interests, who were accused of laying plans to get rid of McSween and Tunstall by fair means or foul. Both sides began to recruit cowboys who could also serve as gunmen.

Young William Bonney, riding light-heartedly along, was bringing assets that would make him acceptable to either party. He was brave, a quick and accurate shot, loyal, and coolly competent in a pinch. Among men he was at ease, but shy with women. Add Casey related that when the Kid first came to their ranch he held back too embarrassed to meet Add's mother and two sisters.

There is no dearth of stories about Billy the Kid; both factions have left advocates and there are at least two versions of every tale. The definitive account of the Lincoln County War awaits the history of Maurice Garland Fulton who has devoted years to scholarly research. Meanwhile one can only pick the version of every tale most consistent with facts too well authenticated for dispute.

Some say that the Kid worked for awhile for Murphy and Dolan; their descendants deny that. In any case, he was soon employed by John H. Tunstall on his Rio Feliz Ranch, and there the cultivated Englishman and the outlawed boy became friends. George Coe, in his *Frontier Fighter,* quotes Tunstall as saying: "That's the finest lad I ever met . . . I'm going to make a man out of that boy yet. He has it in him." One wonders what such a man might have done for the eighteen-year old. But that friendship, probably the purest of the Kid's life, was to make him — so out of

58

joint were the times — a criminal hunted to his death by an officer of the law.

It began because an insurance company in Philadelphia disputed payment of a policy. Colonel Emil Fritz had left Lincoln and returned to Germany. There he died, leaving insurance of $10,000 to his sister and other relatives in Lincoln. The company refused payment on the plea that Fritz had not admitted that he had tuberculosis, and Alexander McSween, as attorney for the Fritz estate, went east to collect.

Mr. McSween left his wife in peaceful Lincoln Plaza, comfortable in her adobe house of eight well-furnished rooms, with her sister for company, books and piano for her diversion, and everybody in town as her friends. She had two Negro servants, George Washington and Seburn Bates, and doubtless Mexican girls to help with the housework. Bates is best remembered because "his big hands brought the sweetest notes out of his guitar." Often Frank Coe, fiddler with dash and style, dropped in to play with them. And when John Tunstall and his cowboys were in town, they called on Mrs. McSween too. The Kid had a sweet thin tenor and he loved to sing, especially *Over the River,* a mournful ballad about how he would never see his love again. Who Billy's true love was is not certain; gossip hints that he loved, unrequitedly, at least two Lincoln girls whose families were too correct to permit more than dancing at the *bailes.*

Bailes were as democratic as the frontier. When Frank Coe and Seburn Bates walked along Lincoln's one street, playing to announce the dance, everybody made ready to attend. No baby was too young, no grandparents too feeble to go along. Often the oldest were the most agile dancers on the hard, well-sprinkled adobe floor. Ladies

wore their best silk, satin, or rep dresses with bustles, flutings, ruch-
ings, and bead appliques: all copied from pictures in eastern news-
papers or magazines. Mrs. McSween's gowns are remembered as
the richest, but none were more exquisitely made than Mexican
ladies could produce with their convent trained hands. And nobody
missed a *baile* for lack of silk. Calico could also be bunched up
most stylishly and many a ball gown was washed and ironed just
in time. Men, lacking formal attire, scrubbed up and came redolent
of laundry soap with bright kerchiefs against their blue wool shirts,
and boots greased to a shine. They wore their guns. Some posted
lookouts. No girl refused to dance with a man because he happened
to be wanted by the sheriff at the moment.

They danced schottisches, polkas, and swift waltzes as all the
frontier did; but New Mexico's dual culture gave them also *La
Cuna, La Raspa,* and *La Varsoviana.* They spoke and sang in two
languages too or in the lingo that was evolving from Spanish and
English. Children did not know which was which, and The Kid
was just as easily *Billicito.* Mannerly, well-washed and well dressed,
full of pranks and a superb dancer he had the added charm of his
reputation as a cool and ready fighter. Girls were glad to be his
partners.

Señora Genoveva Salazar, then Lucero, remembers her first *baile,*
when she was ten and *Billicito* asked her to dance. She held back,
afraid. But her aunt poked her up. *"Baila con el. Es buena gente!
Muy buena gente!"* (Dance with him, he's good folks; very good
folks!) Señora Salazar still considers the Kid the best dancer in
seven counties. She remembers that thereafter she and her sisters
used to work hard all week weeding the beans and chile so their
father would take them to the *baile* on Saturday night.

Little Ella Bolton found Billy almost too good. She also had her doubts about dancing with the outlaw, but accepted. Billy, finding her light on her feet, swung her clear off them, making a picture somewhat like Alice with the Red Queen. When a pause came and he set her down, little Ella stalked away with as much dignity as her small figure and baby face could muster.

Possibly Billy was just as happy dancing with Citroneva Griego who waltzed so smoothly that she could carry a glass of water on her head and never spill a drop. Or with Natividad Montaño, who, according to one account, was engaged to Billy when he was killed. Others indignantly deny any such affair; no family as correct as the upperclass Montaño would have permitted such an alliance for their daughter!

But all was not as friendly in Lincoln as the *bailes*. Mr. McSween's trip east was to lead to tragedy. On his return he reported success to his wife. He had collected $3,053.79, all that remained of Emil Fritz's $10,000 policy after deducting expenses for McSween's trip, his fee and that of an eastern firm of lawyers. The Fritz heirs were not satisfied. By this time, Lawrence Murphy's new partner, Jimmie Dolan, had married one of Emil Fritz' nieces. On the advice of Murphy and Dolan, the heirs brought suit against McSween for embezzlement, and William Brady, Sheriff and Murphy's friend, attached his property — not only the store he owned jointly with Tunstall, but cattle on Tunstall's ranch on the Rio Feliz.

Sheriff Brady sent William S. Morton as his deputy and a large posse to attach Tunstall's cattle. This Morton was the Billy Morton the Kid had known in Las Cruces; other members of the posse were Morton's pal, Frank Baker, and the Kid's boyhood friend,

Jesse Evans. All these men belonged to the Seven Rivers gang and were enemies of Tunstall who had once had them arrested for stealing his cattle. Tunstall's friends think, to this day, that it was a frame-up to drive McSween and Tunstall out of the country, if not to kill Tunstall. Ordinarily it does not take a large posse to serve a paper on a peaceful citizen. The riding of this posse was unknown to the McSweens at home in Lincoln.

Their household had just been enlarged by the arrival of the Reverend T. F. Ealy and his family; Dr. Ealy was the missionary and physician sent in response to Mr. McSween's request. Happily, letters written by Mrs. Ealy at the time have recently come to light and we have a woman's report on Lincoln County at its wildest.

On a cold February day, the Ealys finally drew up at Fort Stanton, after five wearying days of jolting over the rutted roads from Trinidad where the narrow-gauge railroad ended. Mrs. Ealy was so sore and exhausted that she thought she could go no farther. Major Dowlin advised Dr. Ealy to return to "the States"; word had just come in of the killing of one John H. Tunstall. What he told of conditions in Lincoln gave Mrs. Ealy "shivers of apprehension." But Dr. Ealy was eager to reach his new vineyard; Miss Gates, who had come along to open a school, was ready; the children were still agog over Indians and soldiers and not tired at all. So they went on. On the road Mrs. Ealy's shivers mounted into absolute terror when they were stopped and searched for firearms. Mr. Ealy's plea that his cloth be respected brought such scorn for him and such hatred of McSween that the peaceful missionaries knew they were riding into warfare and had met the enemy.

At Lincoln Mrs. Ealy was reassured by the warm welcome of Mrs. Shields, representing her sister, Mrs. McSween who was visiting at Chisum's ranch. In warm, well-furnished rooms, Mrs. Ealy thought she had found rest and peace. But before night a messenger brought news. Sheriff Brady's posse, headed by Billy Morton, had killed Tunstall. Morton said Tunstall had resisted, had shot first. As Tunstall's men had ridden off after turkeys, leaving him alone, this point is still disputed. But the viciousness of the attack was attested by the state of Tunstall's body when they brought it in, lashed to the back of a burro. He had been killed by a shot through the heart; then his head had been riddled by another. Dr. Ealy, as physician, embalmed the body, and, as minister, read the service as they sadly buried young Tunstall behind the house. This was the first of thirty burials Dr. Ealy was to conduct during five months in Lincoln; all but one had been killed.

Alexander McSween, white-faced and stern, but a Christian who behaved according to the tenets of his faith, prayed often but steadily refused to carry a gun. His friends, distrusting this creed of non-violence and counting not at all on law as administered by Sheriff Brady, organized as "The Regulators." Among them was Billy the Kid, his young face white and strained, his mind made up. His friend had been killed; he would kill everybody responsible for that dastardly act, shooting on sight, asking and giving no quarter. Meanwhile life went on somehow in the McSween home, and Mrs. Ealy could report some pleasant happenings.

Miss Gates opened her school, and on Sundays Mr. Ealy preached and Mrs. Ealy played the piano for the hymns. The cowboys often stood around her piano, armed, but singing lustily. The Kid especially impressed her because he knew the hymns; he said he used to go to Sunday school in Silver City. But try as they would to make normal peaceful living, the women knew that warfare was just outside the eighteen-inch adobe walls. Through the lace curtains they saw men walking with Winchesters on their shoulders; the men who frequented the house went off and came again, saying little of what they had been doing.

McSween, proceeding as a lawyer, had got R. M. Brewer, his friend, sworn in as a special constable to seek out and arrest the murderers of Tunstall. The Kid, of course, joined the party, determined to get Morton and Baker. The pursuit led to "Honest John" Chisum's ranch, where the little city of Roswell now stands.

There Miss Sallie Chisum, who had come out to keep house for her uncle, went off into girlish hysterics when she first saw the Kid; he was so different from the "blood-thirsty ogre" she expected. Walter Noble Burns quotes her in his *Saga of Billy the Kid*. "A good-looking, clear-eyed boy . . . I suppose it sounds absurd to speak of such a character as a gentleman, but . . . he was the pink of politeness and as courteous a little gentleman as I ever met." George Coe relates how the Kid, when shooting was imminent, went politely down to the stream where Miss Sallie was washing and escorted her back to safety.

When Brewer's posse got back to Lincoln, they reported that both Morton and Baker had been killed, "running away from the posse." Who fired the fatal shots was never established. George Coe quotes the Kid as saying later, "Of course you know, George, I never meant to let them birds reach Lincoln alive." George Coe and his cousin, Frank, owned small ranches on the Ruidoso and were doing well cutting the fine prairie grass, and selling hay to the forts. They believed McSween was right in his stand against Murphy and they welcomed all his men at their place. The Kid was always at home, both at the Coe's house and in the nearby village of San Patricio.

San Patricio, a peaceful farming community most of the time, had two enemies to fear. Now and then Apaches rode in to rob the barns, drive off the stock, terrorize the people. Equally feared, and for similar reasons, were bandits from Texas. So the citizens posted a lookout on their highest hill. Hourly his musical cry sounded reassurance to men in the fields, women in the houses, and children at play. *"Sen-ti-nel a-ler-to!"* If marauders appeared his cry would warn, *"Apaches!"* or *"Tejanos!"* as he tumbled down the hill to take refuge in barricaded houses and help fight off the enemy.

But when Billy the Kid came everybody was glad. Girls liked to dance with him; so smooth and fast in the waltz, so agile and gay in schottische or polka, so graceful as he twirled his partner about in *La Varsoviana*. And in the morning, when he left and the eager kids were watching and trying to help with bridling and saddling, he would empty his pockets of all loose change for them.

Between these peaceful appearances in the plazas, the Regulators were pursuing their war. Their enemies said they were bound to wipe out all law in Lincoln County. But law, in the person of Sheriff Brady, looked to them like the enemy. On April 1st, the Kid and three others, in Lincoln again, hid behind the adobe wall of McSween's corral. They had dug out the adobe to make loopholes; when Sheriff Brady appeared on the streets they shot him down. Whose shot took effect was never proved. The Kid of course, got the blame. A warrant was sworn out against William S. Bonney, alias Billy the Kid, for the murder of Sheriff William Brady.

John L. Copeland, a fair and honest citizen, was made sheriff, but soon the complaisant Governor Axtell removed him and appointed George W. Peppin sheriff. He was an out and out Murphy man. Mr. McSween took steps to bring the whole affair to the attention of Washington, urging the appointment of another governor. But things in Lincoln moved too fast for Alexander McSween's legally correct processes. Both sides were shooting on sight. Billy's enemies say that the Kid, avenging his friends, was becoming a killer, vicious, without scruple. Colonel Fulton, the most impartial student of the period, says the Kid killed only three men alone. Other killings attributed to him were the result of volleys from many guns. Billy the Kid had become Billy the Scapegoat.

On July 14, 1878, the Regulators — about fifty men — moved silently into Lincoln during a dark night. Martin Chaves, whom they had elected to command, placed them at Montaño's store, Patron's house, and at McSween's, where store and house made a U-shaped fortress, and outhouses gave added cover. Peppin's men had been expecting them at San Patricio, were slow in getting back to Lincoln. That was Sunday.

On Monday morning Mrs. Shields' little son reported that there was to be no school that day. The war was on. Women were warned to stay indoors. All who could left town. Desultory firing all day resulted in no casualties, but the women were running out of water. Peppin's forces allowed them to go to the stream behind the house with their buckets.

On Tuesday the firing was brisker. Mr. Green, running in for refuge, reported a man lying on the hillside. Firing stopped while Dr. Ealy went to bring him in. Women and children came in to stay. The defenders were mostly in the large store; the women tried to keep things going normally for the children.

They heard that Sheriff Peppin had asked Colonel Dudley, commanding officer at Ft. Stanton, for aid; and were sure that the bluecoats would end the killing. Then they heard the Colonel refused to move. His messenger bearing that word was shot. At last, on July 19th, thirty-five enlisted men and all the officers from Stanton appeared before the McSween home. McSween at once asked protection for the women and children beleaguered within. Colonel Dudley replied: "I don't wish any communication with you whatever and if one shot is fired from that house I will open fire from the cannon."

The Colonel did, however, magnanimously permit the removal of Mrs. Ealy, Mrs. Shields and their children to Juan Patron's house, down the street. Mrs. McSween refused to leave her home and her husband. By night the battle was truly joined. The Sheriff's men, ensconced on the hill behind the house, drew fire that way while others, armed with coal oil and pitchpine, built fires against doors and windows. An adobe house burns slowly, but this one burned steadily, hotly, relentlessly on. The men were backed slowly from room to room. Once a bullet struck the piano and brought out a sound of pain. Then they moved it, rolling it heavily over the door-sills.

Mrs. McSween then decided to take a hand. Putting on her bonnet, as a lady should, she stepped out into the street. With bullets falling all about her, she walked directly to where the Colonel sat in his tent, drinking with his friends, Sheriff Peppin and others. She reported to him what was so plainly to be seen. Her house was afire, women and children were in danger; she called upon the US Army for protection. Mrs. McSween was a small woman, but erect of back with flashing black eyes and no fear at all. The Colonel replied that he had no authority to interfere; he was there only in case the civil officers needed help; he thought they had the situation well in hand.

The fire was roaring along faster now. The heat was terrific, the smell of smoke stifling. Coughing, with smarting eyes and flesh beginning to blister, the men fought back from flames; still they moved the piano until it was with them in the last tenable room. The men were ready to surrender. But not the Kid. The youngest, he was the strongest. Holding them with gun and cool, steady eye, he outlined his scheme. On his orders they waited until nightfall and made a dash for it.

The Sheriff's party met them. McSween, still clutching his Bible and praying aloud, was killed. So were three others. Higinio Salazar, left for dead, even kicked to make sure, lay all night motionless while the conquerors celebrated. At dawn he rolled down the hill to the creek and got away to live and tell the tale. Billy the Kid and several others got away.

Colonel Dudley reported that the defenders, as well as the Sheriff's party, had shown remarkable courage. So fair he was, but he was not above besmirching Mrs. McSween's character. But she had shown herself the heroine of that dreadful nineteenth of July, and afterward she showed herself such a fighter as her husband was not. She engaged Huston I. Chapman as her lawyer and prepared to fight to clear her husband's reputation. On February 18, 1878, Mr. Chapman was shot down in the streets of Lincoln by a group including James J. Dolan. The Lincoln County War had not ended. Nor had Mrs. McSween's courage and determination to clear her husband's name and save what she could from the shambles of her home and looted store. She fought on through the courts, won her case. In time she remarried, divorced, and lived to a beautiful and prosperous old age in White Oaks. The "Cattle Queen" they called her.

The Kid's courage, too, brought him a chance to clear his record. Mr. McSween's efforts to proceed legally had at last reached Washington, and President Hayes removed Governor Axtell and appointed General Lew Wallace as Governor of New Mexico. Governor Wallace was busy finishing his *Ben-Hur* in the Governor's adobe "palace" in Santa Fe, but the Chapman murder brought him to Lincoln on a personal investigation. First he needed witnesses not afraid to tell the truth about the Colonel and the Sheriff. William Bonney was recommended as fearless. Governor Wallace wrote a polite note asking him to call.

The Kid appeared at the designated hour, poised in the doorway, his pistol cocked. "I was to see Governor Wallace." "I am Governor Wallace. You have nothing to fear. There is nobody in the house but us." The talk was brief, but satisfactory. The Kid agreed to testify. The Governor, aware that trying to bring murderers to justice would result in arresting every man in the county able to carry a gun, had decided to issue a general amnesty. The Kid did appear in court, as a witness.

It was too late for Billy the Kid, even if he had wished to, to go over to law and order. To the Governor's offer of protection he replied with truth: "Long before I could reach you, General Wallace, they would kill me." In any case Billy the Kid went back to his old ways, more than ever an outlaw, more than ever cattle-thief and killer. Three times he was in jail in Lincoln. Of two occasions he left his own record. Lincoln, having lost several important criminals, had built a jail to hold. It was a hole in the ground, lined with pine logs — floor and walls, and its roof beams upheld the floor of the jailer's house. When Billy was taken there for the second time, he pulled out a pencil and wrote on the door-jamb words that remained until the jail itself disappeared.

"William Bonney was incarcerated the first time, December 22, 1878; second time, March 21st, 1879, and hope I never will be again.

W. H. Bonney"

During one of those visits — her daughters do not remember which — Billy appealed to another good woman. Mrs. Bolton, who had brought her three children from Ireland to join her soldier husband at Fort Stanton, was living in Lincoln when they put the Kid in that underground dungeon. Mrs. Bolton knew his age, knew that dreadful place, like an animal's cage, worried and wondered. Finally she went to see the prisoner, tagged by her two daughters — Minnie, almost grown, and little Ella whom the Kid had swept off her feet in the dance. Neither remembers what was said; only that Mother went back later with doughnuts and hot strong tea for the Kid.

The Kid escaped from that jail, as he did later from the old Murphy-Dolan store building where they had him under sentence of death for the murder of Sheriff Brady. The Kid slipped his handcuffs, killed his guards, terrorized the population and, counting as always on his friends, got clean away.

Some of this is history. It is history that Governor Wallace wrote: "A precious specimen nicknamed The Kid whom the Sheriff is holding here in the plaza . . . is an object of tender regard. I heard music and singing the other night; going to the door I found the minstrels of the village actually serenading the fellow in his prison." It is legend that a girl wished to invoke an old Mexican custom permitting a virgin to offer herself as substitute for a criminal condemned to hang.

Billy escaped from Lincoln. But he could not escape his destiny. He was to be killed in the dark at Ft. Sumner by Pat Garrett who had been appointed Sheriff for that purpose. That was the night of July 14, 1881. The romantic say that the Kid had hung around Ft. Sumner trying to persuade his sweetheart to go with him to Mexico. Certainly he could have gone alone to Mexico and been safe. But here he was in Ft. Sumner at the home of a friend he trusted. Alone, in stocking feet and armed only with a butcher knife, he was coming to cut a steak off a beef carcass hanging in the entry. In the dark he passed two deputies sitting on the porch.

"Quien es?" he asked, walking into the unlighted room where Pat Garrett sat. "Who is it?" as though he wished to know which of his enemies was to get him finally.

Garrett shot, and the Kid fell dead without a word.

Women took charge then. The Navajo Deluvina rushed in with her wail: "They have killed my little boy!" Women laid him out on boards in the carpenter shop, placed candles, prayed and wailed until they buried him next day. When Sister Blandina got the word in Santa Fe she wrote: "Poor, poor Billy the Kid was shot by Patrick Garrett of Lincoln County. That ends the career of one who began his downward course at the age of twelve years by taking revenge for the insult that had been offered to his mother."

4. The Mystery of the White Sands

On a January afternoon in 1896, Colonel Albert J. Fountain was ready to leave his home in Las Cruces for the midwinter term of court in Lincoln, a hundred and fifty miles away. Though it was already four o'clock, the Colonel seemed to be waiting as he stood chatting by the fat base-burner. Its warm glow made the wide hall very cozy, and even took the chill off the parlor which was not much used anyhow. The stately adobe house was furnished in the fulsome taste of the nineties, and adorned with mementos of the Colonel's active life. His legal diploma from Columbia University; the sword he carried as an officer in the California Column just after the Civil War; a hat from Panama, where he had shared in a revolution; fine blankets and beaten silver from

Mexico; trophies from Apache fights; gifts from the Texas Rangers, and from the Masonic lodge he had founded in Las Cruces. In the parlor hung a painting of the Colonel in uniform, very military with keen blue eyes and flowing mustaches. Opposite was a portrait of Mrs. Fountain at thirteen, when she came as a bride from Durango in Mexico. A gentle, big-eyed girl with long ringlets, a high-necked bodice, and a heavy chain and locket. Since then her figure had thickened with bearing eleven children, but her face was still pretty and gentle with the Mexican wife's submissiveness. She was filled with forebodings about this trip.

Frontier women were accustomed to seeing their men off on long trips across lonely country; and any man as active and partisan as Colonel Fountain was bound to have enemies. But this time Mrs. Fountain was unduly nervous; and her apprehensions had augmented the concern of her sons who knew their father's business in Lincoln, and who his enemies were. They said little. The Colonel's decisions were not questioned by his family.

The children had all gathered to see him off, except Mrs. Claussen who lived in Hillsboro. Albert, Jr., also married, had ridden over from Old Mesilla to accompany his father, but the Colonel refused; and Albert, trained in the old tradition, said years later, "My Papa command' me don't go, and of course I had to obey my Papa." Maggie and Katy were the most popular young ladies in Las Cruces — blue-eyed Maggie of pure Spanish type, and dark and vivacious Katy. Tom and Jack, just grown, had put the team into the buckboard and stocked it with blankets, a keg of water, food, the Colonel's dispatch box and grip, guns and ammunition. Everything was ready, but the Colonel lingered.

Then, just before dusk, little Henry came flying in, his dark eyes shining. "I can go," he shouted. "Papa said if I got home from school in time I could go, and I'm here!"

Colonel Fountain was fond of his children, but nine-year-old Henry was the admitted favorite who generally tagged him around town. The boy's small valise was already in the buckboard, so the Colonel kissed them goodbye, sons and all, and pulled on his gloves. The wife clung to her husband, weeping, and at the end she gave him a muffler of her own that he might at least be warm. She did not seem to have feared for her child. Maybe she hoped the boy would somehow be a protection to the man. She saw them drive away, and settled down in her big adobe house to wait, and to pray.

Colonel Fountain represented the new era just beginning in the west. He was for law and order, but he was a fighter too. He had organized the Mesilla Scouts to fight Apaches, he led many a posse, he was a belligerent member of the Republican party, and a pugnacious newspaper editor. As a lawyer, he was dramatic, "a powerful pleader, and the only one who could make a hardboiled Mexican jury cry." In his lighter moments Colonel Fountain wrote plays which he directed, and even acted in. He always went armed, for in spite of college training and settled traditions the old pioneer ways suited his temperament exactly.

Even after Pat Garrett killed Billy the Kid, the struggle continued between men who preferred the old lawless ways and men who advocated the regular processes of the law. Cattlemen registered their brands and hired private detectives to pursue thieves and bring them to court. Rustling became a crime. The New Mexico Stock Association had become a power in politics, and Albert J. Fountain was its lawyer. He fought rustling in his paper as well as in the courts, demanding exposure of men in high office who connived at it. He named names and made himself a formidable collection of enemies. One said: "He was a man who picked up the hates of people."

Las Cruces was in the thick of this fight. It was a flat-roofed adobe town with a couple of two-storied buildings, and a few stretches of board walks above the streets of river sand. Three big general stores served a hundred-mile radius of scattered ranches, and many saloons lubricated business and social life. A majority of the population were Mexicans who knew no English, but who took readily to politics and were generally Republicans, their idea of loyalty being to adhere to the Union party. The hatreds and bitternesses of the Civil War dominated politics, and feeling often flared up into shooting scrapes. The county was normally Republican, with an occasional Democratic victory.

Among the fighting Democrats were the Falls, father and son. The son, Albert Bacon Fall, was destined to a dramatic national career. Sadie Orchard of Hillsboro, who lived by the standards of the eighties, said of him: "I knowed Fall when him and Doheny was a-poundin' a drill up at Kingston; and I don't care what they say about him now, Fall was a man, he was allus a MAN." Vigorous and highly intelligent, Fall rose rapidly from the Kingston miner to district judge, a dominant figure in the territory. Fall and Fountain were enemies, and they were well-matched.

As Fountain left Las Cruces that January day in '96, he must have known that he was a tempting target for men who accepted the frontier ethic that a man's first duty was to protect himself and his friends.

The next day, Mrs. Fountain was thrown into hysterics by the return of her husband's horses, one dragging a rope, the other

76

following. Albert noticed that the halter had been cut and was not soiled. Had someone cut the horses loose and then killed the Colonel? He was just ready to set out when a man arrived with a note from Fountain, saying that his horses had got away, and directing his sons to bring a fresh team to Parker's Wells. They found him where he had made camp for the night. The Colonel showed no concern for his safety, and he still refused to let his sons accompany him.

Nine-year-old Henry said, "Don' be afraid. If anything happens I'll do the shootin', and Papa can do the drivin'."

He and his father got to Lincoln without further trouble.

When they started home again on the last day of January, Colonel Fountain had secured indictments against seventeen men for crimes against members of the New Mexico Stock Association. Among them were "Cause No. 1489; Territory of New Mexico vs. William McNue and Oliver Lee: charge, larceny of cattle"; and "Cause No. 1490; Territory of New Mexico vs. William McNue and Oliver Lee: charge, defacing brands."

Oliver Lee was a young man from Texas who had done well in the cattle business. At this time he owned ranches in the Sacramento Mountains and on the San Augustín Plains. He was a Democrat, a friend of Fall, and an enemy of Fountain. Men divided like that. McNue was one of Lee's cowboys.

On Friday, Colonel Fountain drove from Lincoln to La Luz, stopping only at the Apache Agency where a half-breed gave Henry a little mare.

On Saturday morning, the Colonel was in no hurry to leave La Luz as he could easily make Las Cruces by dark, stopping only to water his team at Luna's Wells and again at Parker's Wells.

With good horses and a light rig, seventy miles a day was not an unusual drive. So he was willing to wait for Miss Fannie Stevenson who had asked for a lift to Las Cruces. While they waited in Charley Meyer's store, Henry asked for candy and his father gave him a quarter. The boy pocketed the change; a nickel and a dime.

John Meadows had observed this and remembered how Colonel Fountain and little Henry went on alone after all. "Miss Fannie," he said, "was a consumptive, and there was a cold wind blowing so she decided not to go. I reckon if she'd a gone, it'd a been different. The Colonel was prob'ly a little more apprehensive than he let on, because he was well-armed, and he carried his Winchester across his knees."

The San Augustín Plains are about forty miles wide there, and as the Colonel's team clopped along, they had the San Andrés Range on their right, and on their left the taller Sacramentos, snow-capped at that season. At the foot of the San Andrés is a long lava bed. Between that and the valley lie the White Sands, which are not sands at all but huge beds of gypsum. Under the winds they heave and shift in heavy glistening waves, forever changing. Anything buried there, even the body of a man, would disappear as though it had been dropped into the sea.

Colonel Fountain stopped at Luna's Wells. Antonio Rey was living there then, and he told afterward that the Colonel seemed worried. As he stood warming his hands before the stove he asked: "Have you seen three men riding by here?"

Rey had seen three horsemen at a distance. "I went out to see if they wasn' comin' in for water, but they wen' a-riding on by. I couldn' see who they was. Better stay here, Colonel, until tomorrow and go back with the mailman."

"No," said the Colonel, "they've been trailing me all day. If they're after me, they'll get me sooner or later and I'm not going to show the white feather. I'll go on." And he did.

The only growth on those plains is greasewood and mesquite not, in that altitude, tall enough to hide a man. A horseman can be seen for ten miles; and as Fountain rode along the three riders kept abreast of him, in plain sight but too far away to be recognized. In those days men exchanged greetings on the trail. If they were going the same way, they joined forces. Fugitives from justice would have ridden over a ridge and so on to Mexico. Only men out for no good would hang on a man's flank like that, too far away for a hail, never approaching, never leaving. At the southern point of the White Sands the road then crossed the line between Lincoln and Doña Ana counties. About there Colonel Fountain met Salurino Barilla, the mailman. He reined up and pointed out his sinister outriders.

Salurino shook his head. "Better you come back with me, Colonel."

One can imagine that by this time the Colonel's fighting blood was up and well-warmed. So again he refused.

"I've got to be in Silver City on Monday," he explained, "and Henry's a little under the weather, so I'll be driving on and get him home to his mama."

The Colonel clucked to his horses, and the buckboard rolled on toward Chalk Hill, a lone small peak sticking up out of the plain. The three horsemen followed.

About sundown on Sunday, February 2, Barilla came to the Fountains' house in Las Cruces.

"Ain' the Colonel here?" he asked.

His story brought consternation. Mrs. Fountain fainted away, and they called a doctor. Her two grown daughters were with her, so Albert and Jack called a group of friends and set off, stopping only for blankets, a little food, and ropes. They did not even notify the sheriff.

The men rode rapidly through Organ Pass and down the long slope to Chalk Hill, where they made camp. As soon as it was light, Albert was up. He pointed out tracks of three horses where it seemed the buckboard had stopped. The men followed those tracks up an old road toward the Jarilla Mountains, and five or six miles from Chalk Hill they came upon the buckboard.

The Colonel's cartridge belt lay on the seat, his cravat hung on one of the spokes of a wheel, and Mrs. Fountain's muffler was folded over the bows of the buggy top. Albert thought these things were a message from his father that he was living then. Everything else was gone: water, provisions, clothing, everything. The Colonel's dispatch box had been opened, and all important papers taken. From that point the trail of five horses led toward the mountains. Near the foothills, the trackers came upon a camp. A big fire had been built there, cans had been opened, and sticks had been used to broil meat. Albert saw the tracks of a man's boot which he measured, and the imprint of a child's shoe. He thought that the small track might have been made by a shoe held in a man's hand. He saw no footprint that he thought was his father's. But he noticed a place where blankets had been laid on the ground with something heavy on them. Bits of wool were caught on the grass, and the weave of the blanket had marked the sand.

Albert spoke to his brother: "Look. A body wrapped in a blanket could have marked the sand like that." And in answer to the younger's shocked face: "They could have fastened a body to a horse with harness straps." The brothers walked on. Beyond that point certainly the marks of one horse's hoofs were noticeably deep in the sand. Perhaps he had carried a heavy load.

Not far from that cold camp, the trails separated. The men easily identified the tracks of a small mare, though they only learned later about the Indian's gift to Henry. That mare had gone north. The heavily laden horse and another bore south. A trail of several horses hit for Dog Canyon Wells, one of Oliver Lee's ranches. The men, separating, followed them all, but none led to Colonel Fountain, nor little Henry, nor their murderers. It was bitter weather. The men were cold and weary and not well supplied with food or water. They begged Albert to go home.

One of them said, "Albert, you will be killed. These men are desperate. If you go on, they'll kill you, sure."

"That's just what I want," said Albert. "I want to see the man who wants to kill me. Then I'll see the man who killed my father, and you'll know who did it."

By evening they had reached a place where a bunch of cattle, driven across the trail, had obliterated it hopelessly. As they stood forlornly considering what to do next, horsemen hove in sight — a posse from Las Cruces headed by Major W. H. H. Llewellyn. They had left Las Cruces soon after the Fountain boys and their friends and had discovered the same clues. But the Major, agile at jumping at conclusions, was satisfied that the trail was going to Lee's ranch, and that the cattle had been driven across on purpose to efface the tracks. Albert did not agree with him, though he admitted that one horse might have gone to Lee's place.

The Major, assuming command, insisted that the grief-stricken

Fountain boys should go home. They were exhausted and their horses were jaded. So they left the trail to their father's friends and rode back to Las Cruces.

The town was in a fever of excitement. The news that Colonel Fountain has disappeared spread like wildfire, and all day Monday men gathered in knots talking vengeance. On Tuesday the *Rio Grande Republican* came out with an extra.

"Justice," said the paper editorially, "has too long been trifled with in this county. The scale has fallen from her eyes, and if the officials whose duty it is to do cannot stamp out crime, then it develops upon the people to take the law into their own hands." The editor's meaning was clear, though he had some difficulty with his English. In a later editorial, he became even more definite. "Men of Doña Ana," he asked, "is this to continue? Assert your manhood and demand your rights. The hour is at hand. The vigilantes enforced the law in the fifties. Why not now?"

After this inspired effort to calm the angry passions, the *Republican* must have felt some regret when it announced that violent excitement had subsided. "But," it added hopefully, "if the searchers find what they are looking for, there will be a battle."

The press of the whole territory took up the case, taking sides according to politics. Republicans accepted Llewellyn's theory of the guilt of Oliver Lee and his cowboys, William McNue and James Gilliland. Democrats insisted that the whole thing was a frame-up to get Fall. Fall, in an interview, said: "Fountain might have been killed, as he had many enemies, but there is no proof that a murder has been committed." Men, not talking for publication, said that Fountain, weary of supporting an extravagant family and a rover all his life, had "voluntarily absented himself." They pointed out that, though he knew he was going into danger, he had refused the company of his grown sons and taken only the child who was his favorite. The horses had not been found. The Mexican border was near. Fountain spoke Spanish like a Mexican, little Henry looked like a Mexican. No bodies were found. As time went on, reports came in of men who had seen the Colonel and his son in places as far apart as Chicago and Mexico City.

Meanwhile, both factions were going armed and there was so much talk of shooting that Governor Thornton went to Las Cruces, offered a reward for the solution of the mystery, and called upon all good citizens to aid the authorities. On February 9, the papers announced another posse which "fully armed and provisioned, will not return until they discover the living or dead bodies of Colonel Fountain and his son."

This posse was headed by Eugene Van Patten, and it was to bring back word of a new and spectacular find. John Meadows of La Luz, who had been doing some trailing on his own, had turned up real evidence. Mr. Meadows told his own tale.

"I'd been under the weather for a week," he said, "and all that week they was lots of talk about Fountain. Everybody mentioned Oliver Lee. Lots of them thought Lee done it, or knew who did. I felt good toward Lee, deep down, and I figured I'd go out as soon as I could, and see."

What Mr. Meadows saw was a pool of blood and several cartridge shells at the place where the buckboard stood. The earlier trailers had missed that clue because it was hidden in tall bunch grass.

"We measured it," Meadows said, "and it was eighteen inches across, and about three inches thick. Blood had sprayed all around.

If a man had been shot there, it might have been as much blood as that. And I found fifteen cents, a nickel and a dime, just like the change Charley Meyers gave the little boy. The next morning I found where two men were handling a horse that was hard to handle. If they were loading a strange pack on a horse, it would act that way, nervous, jumpy."

Meadows bumped into Llewellyn's posse, "which was still millin' round," and the Major expressed his belief that Fountain had been killed by Lee or his men.

"Not God Almighty Himself," said Meadows, "could say that was Lee's outfit, and your sayin' so don't make it so."

In spite of this disagreement, Llewellyn employed Meadows to go on trailing while he and his posse returned to Las Cruces. Meadows spent days following trails: that of the heavily loaded horse that might have carried a dead man; of the small mare that might have been ridden by a living boy; one trail that led in the direction of Lee's ranch; one that had been ruined by a herd of cattle. They all came to the same end: nowhere. Out of them, Meadows evolved a theory.

"East of the White Sands," he said, "in that big lava bed, is an old crater. Once I dropped a heavy stone into it, as heavy as I could lift; and I never did hear it strike bottom. A body could've been dropped in there, and it never could've been found."

Van Patten's news of the pool of blood intensified excitement in Las Cruces to the danger point. The Governor retained Pat Garrett as a private detective, and assured the public that nothing would be neglected to solve the crime. This was the Pat Garrett who killed Billy the Kid — but even he discovered nothing new.

On February 14, Oliver Lee rode quietly into Las Cruces. Many people saw him, sitting erect and relaxed in the saddle, handling his half-wild stallion with hands as light as they were strong. Nobody spoke to him as he pulled up under a cottonwood tree, threw the reins over his horse's head and walked into the sheriff's office.

"I have just heard that there are charges against me, Mr. Sheriff," said Oliver Lee. "Here I am."

The officer was almost too startled to get his feet off the desk, but he managed to stammer, "No, no charges, Mr. Lee."

So Oliver Lee remounted and rode off into the mountains again. Curious that in that town, where many men believed he had committed a heinous crime, where there was hatred and thirst for revenge, nobody would swear out a warrant against Oliver Lee when he came in and asked for it. It is hard to understand why they were so hesitant to cope with that soft-mannered, quiet-spoken young man. But no action was taken until two years later.

By that time, Doña Ana County's Republicans had managed to elect a sheriff who would resign to permit the appointment of Pat Garrett; he would have been hard to elect. Garrett could run down and round up the formidable Oliver Lee, if anybody could.

Meanwhile Lee and his men had been "on the dodge" in the Sacramentos. Lee was courting his wife, he was often at her home, but no sheriff or deputy ever saw him — officially. One day a boy saw a deputy ride up to that ranch house just as Lee was leaving. Lee deliberately pulled on his gloves, swung a leg over the saddle, said "Good day," and trotted off while the speechless officer gaped.

Years later that boy described the Oliver Lee he remembered. "Lee was straight as an arrow then, and slender, and he used to speak so quiet and soft-like, but I knowed there wasn't no better shot nowhere than Oliver Lee, nor nobody quicker with a gun if he had to use it."

In March, 1898, warrants were issued for the arrest of Oliver Lee, James Gilliland, and William McNue for the murder of Colonel Fountain and his son. But it was July before Sheriff Pat Garrett made a determined effort to arrest them.

About four o'clock in the morning of July 12, the Sheriff and four deputies arrived at Lee's Wells. There was a flat-roofed adobe house with a lean-to against it, and a water tank on squared supports. The windmill was groaning gently in the early breeze, and nobody was in sight. As Garrett started into the house he saw a man signalling toward the roof. He and Kearny ran toward the back, while the other men took refuge under the water tower. Kearny dashed up a ladder to the top of the lean-to, and so got his head above the roof. Garrett testified later that both he and Kearny called, "Surrender!" but he admitted that his enthusiastic deputy fired at the same moment.

Lee and Gilliland, asleep on the roof, woke to see Kearny shooting at them. Lee grabbed his gun and fired. Kearny fell. Gilliland fired too, and Garrett was slightly wounded. The two out under the water tower suffered only a deluge of water when somebody cleverly shot holes into it.

"You're a hell of a lot of fellows," yelled Lee, "to order a man to throw up his hands and shoot at the same time."

Garrett was counting his casualties. One man apparently killed, two wounded, two dripping wet under the water tank. He decided to discuss terms. Lee agreed to surrender if he might give bail. He offered Garrett a wagon to take Kearny home, but Kearny died before they got him to Las Cruces. And there was another charge against Oliver Lee.

So the Sheriff and his posse retired, and later Lee, Gilliland, and McNue surrendered to Judge Parker at Las Cruces. The grand jury found indictments against Oliver Lee and James Gilliland for the murder of Colonel Fountain and little Henry. McNue was not indicted.

The defense, pleading that feeling against their clients was strong in Doña Ana County, got a change of venue to Sierra County, thereby staging the trial in Hillsboro, a leafy town in a mountain canyon. Its original outline of flat adobe houses had been pointed up by shingle-roofed residences with scroll trim, as mines were opened in the Black Range and eastern mining and cattle men moved into town. In the nineties, Hillsboro's population numbered about a thousand, and Sadie Orchard and Tom the Chinaman were quite able to feed any stray visitors. But when court opened in May '98, every stage brought in curious folk and partisans who swamped the town. A couple of hundred men brought their round-up wagons and their cooks, and bivouacked under the trees along the river. Mr. Bucher turned over the back room of the bank to the press, and they ran in a special wire to serve the nation's papers.

Ninety witnesses had been summoned, and as many more came to be on hand "in case." Brawny fellows whose spurs clicked as they stalked around with the heavy stride of armed men, and crowded into the court room. They were soft-voiced and courteous as they removed their hats and offered seats to ladies; but they were unaccustomed to this arguing before a quiet gray man in a room where ladies fluttered and whispered.

When the case was called, Judge Parker's first remark was, "Gentlemen coming into court will kindly leave their guns outside." The Judge was quiet-spoken, but back of his judicial calm was a sternness that won respect and obedience. Max Kahler, the sheriff, saw that the prisoners were well guarded in the adobe jail and on their daily walks to court and back. Sadie Orchard sent in their meals, and sympathetic ladies supplied them with flowers.

Richmond P. Barnes, the district attorney, was assisted by William B. Childers, retained by the Masons, and by Thomas Benton Catron, who later sat in the United States Senate and who had volunteered to serve without pay. They were big guns in the Republican party. The defense attorneys were all Democrats: Harvey B. Fergusson of Albuquerque, Harry Dougherty of Socorro, and Albert Bacon Fall of Las Cruces.

An eastern woman who was there, getting her first taste of the West, described Judge Fall: "Slender, handsome in a gypsy way, he was brilliant, flashing, and most impressive. I think his strange power was due to a hint of intellectual insolence and passion."

Of Oliver Lee, she said: "With quick eyes and unobtrusive manners, he carried himself as softly and easily as if he were at a tea party. I was amazed at his low voice and control, and a certain social grace."

James Gilliland was quite young, the typical cowhand, red-handed and gawky.

They spent three days getting a jury. Four jurymen and many witnesses spoke only Spanish, so the trial was lengthened by an interpreter's limping interpolations. Altogether it took three weeks.

When the indictments were read it appeared that Lee and Gilliland were to be tried for the murder of Henry Fountain, nine years old. Colonel Fountain was not mentioned. Oliver Lee, sitting at a table with his counsel, was aghast.

"My God, Fergusson," he said, "they are not accusing me of the murder of the child!"

The prosecution put on dozens of witnesses whose testimony became as confused as the original trail under conflicting stories of a heavily-weighted horse, the blood, the blanket, the print of a high-heeled cowboy boot, and the track of a child's shoe. Fall was at his brilliant best on cross examination. Thomas Branigan, an old Indian scout, testified that he had measured a boot track near the campfire and found the identical track on the roof of Lee's adobe house, and again when he measured McNue's boot. But when defense attorneys asked to see Branigan's copies of those footprints, he gave up; they were lost. Prosecution attorneys had all seen them and they spent a long afternoon asking each other and their clerks where they had gone. They were in a box in the district attorney's office, then they were not. They were gone.

One June 2, the *El Paso Herald* reported that nothing damaging had been shown. Then the prosecution wheeled out their biggest gun: Dr. Francis Crossman of "somewhere back east." Dr. Crossman testified that the pool of gore was human blood. Judge Fall, it appeared, had taken an afternoon off to learn chemistry and he asked questions the doctor did not know were in the book. He flung technical terms around until the interpreter gave up. He finally forced Dr. Crossman to admit that he could not be positive that the sample he had examined was human blood; he just thought so. The *Albuquerque Daily Citizen* disposed finally of Dr. Crossman with the information that he was not even "from the east"; just from Albuquerque.

Pat Garrett provided the crowded court room with a pleasant interlude. On cross-examination, Judge Fall asked him: "What was the condition of affairs when you went to Las Cruces?"

"Oh," answered Garrett, "you fellows had been shooting at one another and cutting up."

"What fellows?"

"You, Lee, and others."

"Why did you wait two years to procure a warrant for the arrest of Lee and Gilliland?"

"You," drawled Garrett, "had too much control of the courts. It was wise to wait."

Judge Fall explained to the Court that his questions were designed to show that the prosecution was not concerned to discover the murderers of Colonel Fountain, but to fasten a crime on the defendants.

Major Llewellyn's appearance as a witness was anticipated with even more pleasure. He did precipitate an exciting interchange, but the real fight was between Fall and Catron. Llewellyn also got mixed up about the boot tracks, and Fall charged him with contradiction. "Didn't you say before—?"

"He did not," said Catron, lumbering up to protect his witness.

Fall, always pugnacious, was on him like a flash. "When you say that, you say what you know is false. You are seeking to post your witness."

Judge Parker's gavel fell and Fall turned, all suavity. "I apologize," he said, "to the Court. I will not apologize to Mr. Catron." And so it stood.

Altogether, the defense played such havoc with the prosecution's witnesses and gave the reporters so many good stories that the

State's attorneys were forced into print themselves. Even while they were presenting their case, all New Mexico papers carried the following box, prominently displayed:

MISREPRESENTATION CHARGED

All newspaper reports, including the Associated Press, sent out from here about the trial of Lee and Gilliland, are gross misrepresentations of evidence and facts generally. We ask you to publish this daily until the trial is over or we notify you that the misrepresentations have ceased.

(Signed) R. P. Barnes, D. A.
Catron and Childers,
Counsel

When the prosecution closed, the defense asked a verdict of not guilty on the ground that, in the absence of a *corpus delicti* no murder had been proved. The court refused to entertain the motion. The ladies of Hillsboro set a large bouquet in front of the defendants. The defense opened.

They stated that they could, if they must, prove that Colonel Fountain was living after the date of his alleged death. But they proposed to prove only that the defendants were at least sixty miles from the scene of the alleged murder at the time it was alleged to have occurred. Witnesses had been coming in on every stage to augment the army camped down by the river. Three of Lee's cowboys, who had been following everything closely, were said to have horses saddled and ready for a get-away in case Lee was found guilty.

The defense introduced only ten of its witnesses; nine men and Oliver Lee's mother. They all testified that Lee was at the home ranch all that fateful Saturday. Mrs. Lee spoke quietly, her face still and white under her sunbonnet. Oliver did not know that he was suspected until days later, she said. Then he told her about it and rode into Las Cruces to give himself up. He was told then that there were no charges against him. He knew, she said, that the Las Cruces paper was trying to arouse enmity against him and so he stayed away.

Oliver Lee went on the stand. Women wept. The court room was silent as the accused man told his story. He admitted that he feared mob violence, but not a fair trial. He had agreed to surrender to Judge Parker, and he had done so. He referred to a letter offering a man $5000 to kill him and Fall. This would have been an effective letter to introduce. Unfortunately, this important letter, like the prosecution's footprints, had been lost. Prosecution and defense were now even. As Lee left the stand there was a soft patting of hands among what the papers called "the gentler sex." The Judge sternly put a stop to that.

The arguments took days and are still cited as among the most brilliant in the legal history of the southwest. The *El Paso Herald* reported: "Mr. Fergusson's style commands attention. He talked straight to the jury as individuals, sometimes calling the men by name. He said that no evidence had been presented to prove that anybody had been killed or was dead. He confined himself to the evidence presented by the prosecution because their witnesses had so strengthened the defense 'that we dismissed most of our witnesses and all our doctors.' He hinted at the use of bribery and ended that 'Colonel Fountain, who was the soul of honor, would not have lent himself to such methods as have been used to make a case against these two young men.'"

Fall, in summing up, made such an impression that nobody who heard him ever forgot it. His manner was easy and most commanding, and his low voice vibrated like a violin string in the packed and silent court room. He demanded a verdict of first degree murder or acquittal. "I ask for no mantle of charity for these men, I desire no vindication. I ask simply stern justice. If the evidence in this case convinces you that these men murdered little Henry Fountain, you must convict. If you are not convinced, turn them loose. There is no alternative."

Judge Parker did not agree. He charged the jury that they might find the defendants guilty of first, second, or third degree murder; or not guilty. It was half-past eleven at night. The crowded court room relaxed, stirred, whispered. It was said that if the verdict was "Guilty", there would be shooting. It was said that the jurymen had ordered their horses for midnight.

Before that time the jury returned. The verdict was "Not guilty!"

The Judge, quiet but stern, prevented any demonstration as he instructed the sheriff to hold the prisoners for the September term of court. They would then stand trial for the killing of Deputy Kearny at Lee's Wells.

Both these indictments were later dismissed, and nobody ever stood trial for the killing of Colonel Fountain.

For years New Mexico was filled with rumors about Colonel Fountain and little Henry, with whisperings of people who knew just what had happened. But most of these eager wiseacres are now dead, as are all the principal actors in that stirring drama. Only the mountains and the great empty basin of the San Augustín Plains remain as they were. They and the shifting heavy waves of the White Sands keep their secret well.

5. How Black Jack Lost His Head

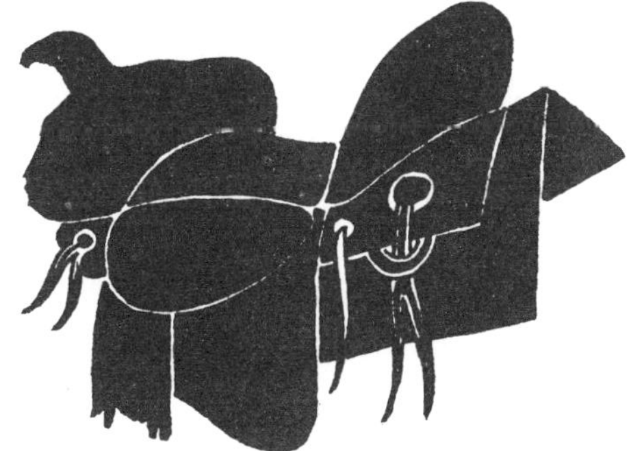

Cimarron was a tough town in the nineties. On the through stage route from Trinidad in Colorado, to Ft. Union, Las Vegas and Santa Fe, it lay close to the mountains, convenient for easy disappearances up the canyons. It was the center of the long bloody feuds of the Maxwell Land Grant, night riders might be anybody, anybody looking innocent and seeking a job as a "hand" might be a wanted man. It was not polite to ask a man's name. "How do you call yourself?" was the correct form.

Jim Hunt, running a store in the old Maxwell ranch house, noticed strangers in town, off and on. He observed that they did not seem to be doing enough business nor saving enough money to account for the twenty dollar gold pieces they used in their games among themselves. Nor for the hundred dollar bill they asked Henri Lambert to change. Henri certainly had the change, but he said he did not, shrugging in his French way and going back to the cooking that made his St. James Hotel famous. Mary Lail, who was a girl then on the Ponil, remembers that a fellow called Bronco Bill used to show up at their dances; he danced well, they asked no questions. One of the strangers who bought provisions, in different stores and in small lots, called himself G. W. Franks. Heavy-set, light, squint-eyed, and with his hat pulled down, he was a saturnine character with nothing to say. He was later identified as Will Carver. Then there was a tall, sandy, and remarkably ugly man who appeared now and then. Cowboys, riding the canyons on their regular business, knew that these men were camped in Turkey Canyon, a rough, narrow slit in the ridge; but they reached their hide-out not along the road, but by the longest way up the Cimarron and down Turkey Canyon. Hankins, driving stage up from Springer, brought in a good many boxes of ammunition for that camp. Mr. Hankins had been sworn in as a Wells Fargo messenger and he knew what he carried. Altogether folks in and around Cimarron noticed a good deal; but they did not say much, even among themselves. Jim Hunt wrote to the neighboring sheriffs that he thought these strangers might bear watching.

Now and again news came in by stage or rider of hold-ups here and there throughout New Mexico. The Atchison, Topeka and Santa Fe had been robbed in a lonely spot near Grants. The Southern Pacific was boarded west of El Paso, in that wild country the Apaches used to range. But mostly the Colorado and Southern suffered, where it angled across the short grass country of northeastern New Mexico to connect Colorado and Texas. Near Folsom, where the tracks made an S on the grade climbing up from the Dry Cimarron to the plain, was the favored spot. They soon were calling it Robbers Roost.

Those robbers, whoever they were, were after express. With few banks in New Mexico, ranchers and store-keepers paid not by check, but in cash; and money was shipped in by express. A car loaded with boxes and bags of silver and gold was tempting loot; and one messenger, armed but wishing to live, was not hard for two men to overcome while their friends held off the engineer and fireman.

The New Mexico Territorial legislature had done its bit, egged on by railroad attorneys who attended every session and did even more persuasive business at the popular saloon known as "The Capitol." Wherever he was, whatever he did, the New Mexico politician was at The Capitol and attending to business. On February 9th, 1887, a bill was introduced in the Council, the upper house, "declaring certain crimes capital felonies." On February 15th it became law by unanimous vote of eleven members, including Mr. President. Only one was absent. The law provided, with typical legal repetitiousness, the death penalty for anyone who should wilfully . . . "assault any train, car, or locomotive with intent to commit robbery, murder, or any other felony upon any engineer, brakeman, conductor, mail or express agent, or passenger." It seemed a law sure to deter ambitious robbers from attacking trains. The only trouble was that, as in making rabbit pie, you had first to catch your robber. Train robberies went merrily on, but robbers consistently escaped.

Often, when the bandits were not caught, Black Jack Ketchum was named; Black Jack's gang was notorious, almost ubiquitous, and perhaps accused of more than it did. Likely more than one man figured as Black Jack. Ketchum was known as having worked cattle in Texas. John H. Culley, in *Cattle, Horse, and Men,* describes a handsome fellow who showed up at the Bell Ranch. He was tall, finely built, wearing a square black beard and a gun he never parted with, day or night. The boys decided he was a "tough hombre," but they enjoyed watching him twirl his gun on his trigger finger, cocking and firing with astonishing speed and accuracy. Only after he left did a deputy sheriff, looking for a hold-up man, tell them they had been entertaining Tom Ketchum, the fearsome Black Jack.

The deputy said that a little store at Liberty, near the Bell Ranch, had been held up by two men. The proprietor, Levy Herztein, riding in pursuit with more pluck than judgment, was killed as he neared their camp. Nobody doubted that Black Jack was the man they sought, but nobody caught him.

On September 3, 1897, the Colorado and Southern's southbound passenger train was held up on that long S curve five miles south of Folsom. As the train labored on the grade, a man stepped into the engine from the tender and ordered the engineer to stop the train. This one was Black Jack. As the train stopped he made for the express car as two other bandits appeared, Will Franks and Sam Ketchum. Will McGinnis was left holding the horses. The express messenger refused to open the safe, saying he did not know the combination. Black Jack knocked him out with the butt of his rifle and in the ruckus a sack broke spilling silver dollars on the floor. Sam gathered them up, Black Jack warned off Conductor Frank Harrington running forward with his lantern, and the men got away. Dixon, the rear brakeman had dropped off and gone back to Folsom to report. Posses were quickly gathered, but the gang had made a clean get-away with some $3,500.

So far as anybody knows Black Jack himself never appeared in Cimarron. His name was associated with holdups in Arizona, and for a couple of years New Mexico was calm. Then, in the spring of 1899, a gentlemanly young man came into Cimarron with a string of cattle from the WS Ranch and registered at the St. James. He soon moved out to the camp in Turkey Canyon. To this day he remains a mystery man. Miguel Antonio Otero, in *My Nine Years as Governor,* identifies him as Ezra Lay. He was known as Will McGinnis, even to the courts. How he came by his refined ways was never explained.

In July, word was brought that the Colorado and Southern's crack train, the Denver-Ft. Worth Express, had been held up again at that favored spot near Folsom. The technique was the same; one man boarded the engine, stopped the train, ordered engineer and fireman out and held them while his partners dealt with the express messenger. Tellers of this tale differ as to what loot the robbers got. The most amusing story is that the express messenger, quick and resourceful, dropped the money bags behind some fruit boxes and that the bandits found only 2 crates of lemons and a pack saddle. All the trainmen were new to this except Conductor Harrington who found himself figuring in the second hold-up in the same place.

Frank Harrington's friends began to guy him about his "pals", the train robbers, and Conductor Harrington bought himself a sawed-off shot gun and kept it handy.

The day after that second hold-up, a teamster brought word into Cimarron that he had been roused in the early dawn by three men riding past where he was sleeping under his wagon. They did not hail, a notable omission, but he thought he recognized them; and as a light rain had fallen, it was easy to trail them up toward Turkey Canyon.

Officers soon appeared in Cimarron. Ed Farr, Sheriff of Huerfano County, Colorado, and James H. Morgan and Captain Thacker, both special agents employed by the Colorado and Southern Railroad. With Jim Hunt's aid they organized a posse and started for Turkey Canyon, going as the gang did, up the Cimarron and down into the narrow ravine. There Sheriff Farr divided his forces. Cimarron men, headed by H. N. Love, a cowboy from Springer, crept along the canyon's south wall. Sheriff Farr with young F. H. Smith, a Chicago lad seeing the Wild West, followed the northern. Soon they saw a campfire through an opening in the thick brush. As they watched a man came down to the little stream with a coffee pot. Will McGinnis. Farr shot, and McGinnis fell. Sam Ketchum ran toward Farr, dropped behind a log and fired. But Farr got him first; his shot shattered Ketchum's right shoulder. But somebody got Farr with a shot that penetrated a large tree where he had sheltered and pierced the man's heart. The bandits evidently had the new high-powered, steel-jacketed rifles.

The special officers had had enough. They knew they had wounded Sam Ketchum and thought they had killed McGinnis, but as they were retiring they saw a rider mount the rise, waving his hat. They recognized McGinnis, who shouted "Adios!" and disappeared over the hill. Will Franks, well ambushed, had kept on firing until dusk when the posse all headed for Cimarron.

Next day they picked up their dead: Sheriff Farr and Cowboy

Love. Two others had been wounded. All three bandits had escaped. But by noon, word came in from the McBride ranch at Ute Park on the Cimarron.

Mrs. McBride, the messenger said, had been alone there with her children when a stranger rode up. A big ugly fellow he was, with a broken arm. Mrs. McBride sent for Pearl Claws, working far from the house, and he got the man to bed. But Claws was suspicious and as soon as he could he sent word to Cimarron that he had caught one of the train robbers. That afternoon, when a deputy sheriff rode up, Claws was sitting beside his patient, chatting amiably. He had picked up the gun and was showing it to one of the McBride youngsters. So it was an unarmed man the deputy arrested.

In Cimarron, when they paused at Jim Hunt's store Jim asked the prisoner who he was. "Who do you think I am?" asked the plug-ugly. "I think you're Sam Ketchum." "Yes," he replied, "I am." Then, gritting his teeth, he added: "But I'm not the meanest man you know. There's a man meaner than me." He indicated Claws. Most men who knew Claws agreed, and still do. According to the ethics of the time and place only "a low-down skunk" would arrest an unarmed man lying down.

Ketchum sat in the spring wagon beside the special officer, who carelessly left his gun on the seat. Young George Crocker, goggle-eyed not to miss a move, saw the prisoner eyeing and edging at the gun, his wounded left arm hampering him. George shouted, "Grab that gun," and did so himself. Crocker remembers that Sam had leaned toward him; he thinks he might have intended to whisper a message for his partners in Turkey Canyon, but the boy was more eager to keep the gun away from the prisoner than to hear his confidences. So that chance was missed. Men were muttering that they would not allow Sam Ketchum to leave town until there had been a trial, but nobody interfered as the rig drove off, taking Ketchum to Santa Fe where he was safely lodged in the penitentiary.

McGinnis and Franks were still on the loose, though rumors came in from all around. Campfires had been seen, a woman on a lonely ranch had fed a man she thought was Will Franks; but nobody who remembered how that fighter had held off ten men in Turkey Canyon was eager to try conclusions with him. It was a relief to the whole countryside when somebody reported seeing Franks and McGinnis riding south.

Tom Ketchum, Black Jack, had taken no part in the Turkey Canyon fight; he had never been seen around Cimarron and had made no move to help his men, unless a ragged cowboy who flashed a roll of twenties in Springer had come from Black Jack with money to defend his brother Sam and the others. The ragged one was Charles Collins; he as good as admitted that he had been with Black Jack's gang and boasted that it would be easy to hold up another train on that grade near Folsom. "Come along," he said, "and I'll show you how easy two men can do it!" He did not suggest that one man might do it. Nobody thought one man could.

More than a month later word came in from Eddy County, down in the southeast corner of New Mexico that Sheriff M. Cicero Stewart had caught McGinnis. Tipped off by a rancher named Lusk, Stewart had apprehended McGinnis as the bandit walked confidently up expecting to meet Franks. Will Franks, the cautious, saw the capture and disappeared without a trace. Doubtless he lived out his life somewhere, calling himself something else.

Jim Hunt, deputized for the purpose, went down and brought back McGinnis, who stood trial for the murder of Sheriff Farr and H. M. Love. McGinnis was defended by a lawyer paid by cowboys. His defense was that he had carried no rifle as he went down to the stream for water and that Farr's shot had knocked him out before he could draw his pistol. He refused to say anything to incriminate himself or others. Altogether his debonair bearing so impressed the jury that they found him guilty of second degree instead of first degree murder as the prosecution had asked. Governor Otero, as he relates in *My Nine Years as Governor,* thought the man had never had a fair trial and after he had served part of his sentence in the penitentiary, the Governor pardoned him.

So ended the Battle of Turkey Canyon. It might have been the end too of the gang. But Black Jack, its leader, was still at large and to be heard from again.

On August 16, 1899, a stranger came into Kent's Saloon in Folsom. A conspicuous stranger, tall and well-built, with black eyes and mustache, dressed well in black clothes and a wide black hat. The habitues gave him a wide and respectful berth, but watched closely as he played. Consistently the wheel ran against him until he had lost about $1,000. Nobody doubted that the player was Black Jack Ketchum, nor that when he left in the early dark he was in need of ready cash.

At 10:15 that night, first class train number 1 left Folsom. Conductor Frank Harrington noted the time as he swung aboard the last car with his lantern. Twenty minutes late. Engineer Joseph Kirchgrabber, up in the engine cab, glanced at his watch too. Four miles out, as the engine labored for the grade Kirchgrabber, keeping a look-out ahead, felt a poke under his arm. Jerking round he saw a tall dark man. Black Jack and no other. With his Winchester, the robber had covered both engineer and fireman.

"What's this?" queried Kirchgrabber, quite unnecessarily.

"It's a hold-up . . . No, don't stop here! Go on till I tell you . . . Stop where the last hold-up was . . . Now get down here and uncouple the baggage car." Still covered, Kirchgrabber and the fireman complied. Kirchgrabber moved slowly; he was naturally a slow-moving man.

"Hurry up there! You son-of-a-bitch! I'll kill you."

In the baggage car the express messenger, Charles Drew, was awake. In the combination and mail car next, Fred Bartlett had got his mail ready and was dozing. As the train slowed he thought it was for Des Moines where he had a sack to toss out. Jumping up, he slid the door open and stood silhouetted in the light from within. A man on the ground with a gun shouted: "Take your damned head in or I'll shoot it off." At the same moment he shot and Bartlett fell, bleeding profusely.

Kirchgrabber and the fireman were struggling to uncouple the baggage car. The coupling, due to the weight of the train on the grade, was locked tight. Perhaps the engineer was not making all the haste he could; as Black Jack cursed, "I'm going to shoot to kill pretty soon," Kirchgrabber replied calmly, "Now partner, we can't do these things all at once," and to the fireman, "Tom, go get me that jackbar off the engine."

This was the delay that foiled the daring attempt at a one-man hold-up. He had picked the wrong spot.

By now, Conductor Harrington, warned by the unscheduled stop, was running forward through the cars, followed by the brakeman, R. B. Hawkins. He got there just in time to hear Black Jack's shout to the mail clerk, and Bartlett's cry as he fell. Harrington ran at once to the train box for the sawed-off shotgun he had so forehandedly acquired, turned off the lights with a key and ran back. Fred Bartlett was crawling in through the door, groaning and bleeding; his face seemed shot away.

"I'm dying," he moaned. Harrington took only time to direct Hawkins to look after the wounded man and dashed for the door.

Drew, the express messenger, was running toward him. He saw the two train men working at the coupling and covered by the robber's Winchester. Harrington shot at once; so did Black Jack, but his shot passed into the mail car where it ricocheted from a post, passed through an empty mailsack hanging on a line and dropped harmlessly to the floor. Harrington's shot had apparently taken effect, for Black Jack disappeared. He must have rolled down the embankment. Mr. Harrington did not investigate, for he heard firing from the other side of the train and thought there was a whole gang about. Nevertheless he walked bravely around, looking, and when he saw nobody he blew four blasts on the engine whistle, the signal for the train crew to come aboard. That brought back Kirchgrabber and Scanlon who had ducked under the train as soon as Harrington's shot knocked the robber out, and had fired those shots at random. They now set to to repair the air-brake hose, broken as they worked with the bar, and to heat the engine up again. Harrington took a turn about with his lantern, but saw nobody, no blood, no sign of struggle. He thought the robbers had got away.

As the train went on, Brakeman Hawkins gave what care he could to poor Fred Bartlett who was suffering extreme pain. Several teeth had been shot out, and his face was to carry disfiguring scars all his life. Conductor Harrington was making up his report. He had, at least, proved that his trains were held up through no connivance of his, and that his foresight in buying that shot-gun had paid off.

The next morning, August 17, the north-bound freight train carried, in addition to its regular crew, Sheriff Saturnino Pinard, a posse from Clayton, and two of the railroad's special officers. Where they hoped to see something, on that grade out of Folsom, they spied a man's black hat, waving. As the train slowed down, Sheriff Pinard jumped down and saw a man, sitting on the ground. He seemed to be resting on a rifle and struggling to pull it out.

"I wouldn't do that, Partner," said the Sheriff. "Where is your other gun?"

"Under my leg, I can't get it." Pinard picked it up.

"The other?"

"I haven't got any other. That's all I had." Then, as the men touched his arm, "Don't do that; it hurts me."

His right arm was tied up in a black silk kerchief, blood soaked; his shirt front was stained with blood, his face drained white and tense with pain. Almost sobbing he said, "I wish that SOB had shot me through the head or the heart. Then all this would be over with." That was the last sign of weakness the prisoner was to show. He was too weak to walk, so they carried him on a cot to the baggage car and left him in charge of Joseph E. Robbins, the rear brakeman, who got a good deal of his story as the train ran on toward Clayton.

The prisoner gave his name as George Stevens; said he would not do anybody any harm; he just needed a few hundred dollars to take him to South America. He told of a sister and brother, decent church-going people in the Panhandle and asked Robbins to take them word if he died. If he did not die he did not want them to know. He again gave the name of Stevens. He also told where he had hidden dynamite for blowing up the train.

Officers found the dynamite later, just where he said it was, under a cattle-guard. There was a picketed horse there too, a pack-saddle with a roll containing a frying pan, a coffee pot, and a Navajo blanket. It was a one-man hold-up all right. And well planned, except for that miscalculation about the couplings that had locked on the grade.

At Clayton Dr. Slack gave first aid; while men and boys crowded around to see the man they were sure was the notorious Black Jack. He was a pitiful sight with several days growth of beard, face white as paper and glassy eyes. On the doctor's advice, Sheriff Pinard decided to take him on to the nuns' hospital in Trinidad. There they removed forty-two shots from that arm, but could do nothing for the shattered bone. After nine painful weeks, Stevens, as he still called himself, was moved to the penitentiary at Santa Fe for safe keeping.

Mrs. Bursum, wife of the warden, remembers coming down the stairs in a fresh dimity party dress as they carried the new prisoner in on a stretcher. His skin was so white, she said, and his hair and eyes so black that he looked like the stage villain of his era. She paused on the stairs and he flashed her an impudent grin as they bore him through the steel doors. That impudence did not desert him even when Dr. Des Marais, the prison physician, amputated the arm. "George Stevens" refused an anesthetic, gritted his teeth, and came through with enough spirit to joke with the doctor. "I hope, Doc, I can do as much for you some day."

Because "George Stevens" had not been fully identified, Sheriff Shields of San Angelo, Texas was asked to have a look at him. His recognition was immediate. Tom Ketchum it was, wanted in Texas for cattle stealing and at several points in New Mexico for train-robbery and various other offenses. It was decided to put him on trial at Clayton, Union County, for the hold-up near Folsom on August 16, 1899.

Black Jack Ketchum was the first train robber to be indicted under New Mexico's severe law providing the death penalty even for an attempted hold-up. There had been previous trials, but as train robbery was a federal offense involving United States mail or express, it was customary to indict under a federal statute that did not carry the death penalty. As New Mexico was a territory, federal cases were brought in the territorial courts, the judge sitting as a federal judge and the district attorney prosecuting as a federal officer. But the record of Black Jack's gang, with three holdups within two years, convinced Governor Otero, and the judges concurred, that it was time to invoke the sterner law and end such effrontery. So Thomas Ketchum, alias Black Jack, was indicted under the territorial law and tried in the District Court at Clayton in Union County.

Judge William J. Mills presided and, upon the prisoner's declaring that he had no money to employ counsel, he appointed William B. Bunker to defend. As Mr. Bunker and his client retired into an adjoining room to confer, a solicitous court attendant closed the door upon them. At once Mr. Bunker popped out. "Here, you, don't leave me alone with this fellow. Somebody come in here with me."

Mr. Bunker did his best. He tried to get a lighter sentence on

108

the plea that the New Mexico law, providing hanging as the penalty for attempted train robbery, was unconstitutional. But the jury found the defendant guilty and he was sentenced to hang. Mr. Bunker appealed to the territorial Supreme Court, and Black Jack was remanded to the penitentiary for safe keeping.

There he was held for more than a year, an exemplary prisoner. His respectable church-going brother from Texas called once, but Black Jack declined to see him. He told Warden Bursum that it was this brother who had started him and Sam on their criminal career. He had planned their first job, left the younger boys to be arrested and departed with the swag to set himself up in respectability.

A more welcome visitor was six-year-old Miguel Antonio Otero, the Governor's son. Often called upon to sign a pardon or a parole, Governor Otero liked to know the men whose lives depended on his word and he made a point of visiting criminals in the penitentiary. Frequently he took along his small son. Miguel Junior remembers his first call on Black Jack in the death house. The desperate holdup whose fearsome record the child knew, was sitting on his heels, cowboy-fashion. He looked up with piercing black eyes, smiled, and spoke politely. His right sleeve was tucked emptily into his pocket, but he could roll a cigarette with one hand and crack peanuts with ease. Young Mike liked to take him peanuts. Black Jack asked the boy to carry messages to the Governor. "You tell your papa not to send me to Clayton. You tell him I'll go straight." The child used to bear the messages faithfully, urging his friend's case and advancing his opinion that the criminal had reformed. But the Governor refused even that plea; Mike could only take peanuts to his friend; never a pardon.

The Supreme Court, after reviewing the testimony, upheld the decision of the District Court and Thomas Ketchum, alias Black Jack, was sentenced to hang at Clayton courthouse on April 26, 1901. The officers who took him there from Santa Fe were fearful of an attempted rescue; they changed trains not only at Lamy where all passengers had to change then, but also at Glorieta and again at Las Vegas. But Black Jack's gang, if they knew what was happening to their leader, made no attempt at rescue. Black Jack maintained an attitude of defiant humor. He had a new black derby, set rakishly on his shining black hair, his mustache was parted and combed, he joked his keepers and the crowds who came to see him. At one station, where cameras annoyed him, he suddenly pulled his shirt up over his head and offered to permit a snapshot for a quarter. He was delivered safely at the Clayton jail. From there on the affair was not quite so conventional.

The hangman, building his scaffold to assure a workmanlike job and a quick and sure death, had made the platform with a drop of eight and a half feet, though the law specified seven. He was allowing for the man's weight; Black Jack was tall and heavily built and he had put on fat in the penitentiary. Black Jack was composed. Only once did he show irritation; on the execution morning he growled: "Why don't they hurry? I'd like to eat dinner in hell." But he was serene as he walked to the scaffold, with his hair combed back, his mustache newly trimmed, his black eyes as defiant as ever. He refused the spiritual ministrations of a Catholic priest and mounted the thirteen steps alone. The black hood was pulled over his head, already in the noose, and pinned securely to his coat; pinned with heavy horse-blanket pins.

"Ready?"

The prisoner himself responded, "Let her go!"

Go she did. The trap was sprung and the heavy body dropped with such force that the head was jerked clean off the body. Blood spurted. The black clothes and black hood were stained an ugly brown and the head would have rolled away if it had not been held by the hood so firmly pinned to the coat. No man who saw that ever forgot it.

It was long held that the hanging of Black Jack put a stop to train robberies in New Mexico; this was cited as proof that stern laws are a deterrent to crime. But in 1937 two young Easterners who had read about Billy the Kid and yearned to be desperadoes held up the Southern Pacific train near Las Cruces. Passengers resisted, and in the melee one of the young men shot and killed a man. They were overcome, promptly arrested and put on trial at Las Cruces where they pleaded guilty to second degree murder. One can only assume that they had not read up on New Mexico's statutes. One must also assume that the court deliberately disregarded a certain statute, as there was no mention of the death penalty. Nonetheless there has not been another attempted hold-up in New Mexico.

6. A Navajo Killing

Peter Parquette sat in his office at Ft. Defiance, New Mexico, expecting a typical day in the life of an Indian Agent. The Arizona sun brought out splotches of purple on the red sandstone cliffs. The usual quota of slim-legged Navajos sat against stone walls, sunning and waiting. Their horses sagged over dropped reins, waiting. Neither man nor horse was waiting for anything in particular. Pete Parquette knew that. As Indian Agent, he knew that if anything ever did happen for or to the Navajos it would have to come a long circuitous red-tape trail from Washington. As part Indian himself, he knew that nothing white men did accomplished anything real for Indians. Even his years in Indian schools and of dealing with whites had not altered that basic Indian fatalism. He gave a push to a pile of papers. He thought of words he might write to add to the long trail of red tape. The January sun was moving softly, trying to reach patches of snow that still hid in the cliff shadows. Nothing was going to happen.

The door opened and a blanketed Navajo stood there. His moccasins had made no sound. "Cross Canyon store is burning," he said.

"What!" Parquette's white training came out in the usual "When? How? Who?" Especially what of Frank Dugan, manager of the Cross Canyon Trading Post. But the Navajo would tell nothing more. Passing, he had seen the store burned to the ground, but still smoldering. He did not go near; Navajos always shy away from a place of death. If an Indian does not want to talk, he won't; so Pete Parquette saved his breath for other things.

First he rang the wall phone, giving the longs and shorts of Mr. Charles C. Manning's store in Gallup, thirty-four miles away. Mr. Manning owned the Cross Canyon post. Soon his soft Virginia accent came over the wire. His first question too was: "What about Frank? Did the man see Frank?" Mr. Manning was fond of Frank Dugan, a young man handicapped by the loss of one hand, but making good with his first trading post. "I'll send Sabin and Mahan right out," he said, "Let me know if you learn anything more."

Parquette, whose duties as Indian Agent included the investigation of crime, made plans to interview Navajos. For some reason he did not go at once to Cross Canyon.

The news was flashing across the reservation, as word runs among primitive peoples, as fast as along wires. By night Navajos a hundred miles from Cross Canyon would be talking. What their comments would be, no white man knew. Even as Pete Parquette pondered his next move, the mailman had reported the burning to the Hubbell Trading Post at Ganado, Arizona, twelve miles from Cross Canyon. Also a Navajo, the mailman had seen nothing either — except the smoking ruins that might, of course, contain a dead body.

One Hubbell son looked at the other. "Remember what the old man used to say? Wonder what they'll find?"

"If Frank is dead, they'll find his head bashed in."

Don Lorenzo, they remembered, used to say that when Navajos killed a white man it was because they needed a scalp. Always, he had said, a secret ceremony followed a killing — especially the killing of a white man. Don Lorenzo Hubbell had been the earliest trader to the Navajos; nobody questioned his knowledge of the people. He suggested that a medicine man might occasionally need a white scalp for ceremonial purposes. Perhaps Navajos had changed since the old trader's day; perhaps not.

All that bitterly cold afternoon of January 17, 1922, Charles Sabin and George Mahan jounced roughly in a Ford along desert tracks that passed for roads. When they reached St. Michaels, twenty-six miles out from Gallup, Sam Day met them. He had the news. A relative of his Navajo wife had brought it. It was too late to do anything at Cross Canyon that night. The men from Gallup accepted the Days' offer of beds for the night.

In the long livingroom of the adobe house Sam's mother made them welcome. She enjoyed company, but she said little. From her rocker by the murmuring base-burner, she directed Sam's Navajo wife who silently moved the oil lamp and the cruet stand and laid more knives and forks on the red table cloth. Mother Day rocked and knitted, her feet on a hassock made of a fine old Navajo blanket. The dusty floor was covered four or five deep with others that would make a museum man gasp.

The men continued their talk. "Might have been only robbery," said Charles Sabin.

"I don't agree with you," countered George Mahan, a younger man, a-quiver with the case. "Navajos kill easier than a white man does because they don't value human life. I heard a Navajo, mad and drunk say: 'If I kill you, what do I get? One year of good food.' "

"It's a fact," said Sabin, "that no Indian ever served more than six years in the pen for killing a white man; I don't believe they've ever hanged even one . . . Of course, if they kill another Navajo . . . But who ever hears about those cases?"

Mrs. Day spoke. "Nobody ever did understand Navajos." Her son said nothing, smoking quietly in his tilted chair. A small, spare man, his fair skin was tanned as leather is tanned, drawn taut over the bones. He did not look at his Navajo wife. She was carding wool in the corner; saying nothing, hearing everything.

Sabin agreed with Mother Day. "Yes, Ma'am, Navajos just don't think like white men. What seems a crime to us, may not be to them. I don't believe they've ever accepted our law as theirs. They'll protect each other."

"So how do we catch this chap who burned the store and maybe—?" Mahan's mind kept returning to killing. The other men said nothing. They were considering the difficulties of tracing a fugitive among forty-thousand Navajos, indifferent if not opposed to their efforts, and across a reservation of 25,000 square miles, wild, mountainous, waterless. They did not even try to make a plan. Dully they turned in for the night on piles of sheepskins.

Sabin and Mahan made an early start. Sam Day, Deputy US Marshal, would follow later. Without him, the other men talked more freely, recalling cases of murder. Young Pat Smith, who kept the trading post at Pueblo Alto while his brother was off at war, was found with his head crushed by a heavy rock, his body soaked with kerosene and burned. Charles Hubbell, killed in 1917 at Tol-Chaco, was beheaded. So was "Sloppy" Jack Lewis, murdered at Peach Springs. Young Mahan shivered to recall that a crowd of drunk and whooping Indians had been seen kicking George Kyle's head like a football; he was murdered in George Sampson's store in 1901 or '02. The Navajo refusal to touch a dead body breaks down hideously in case of murder.

Sabin nodded. "Mother Day is right. Nobody understands Navajos. But maybe there was no murder here. There was plenty in the store to tempt a thief. Remember, just last Friday we shipped Frank nine hundred pounds of flour and twelve hundred of sugar. He must have had at least a thousand dollars' worth of jewelry . . . He may turn up yet, you know."

Mahan shook his head. "Frank was always a little afraid of Indians. That's why he had that white fellow living with him . . . And, come to think of it, that guy was in Gallup Friday. Frank was there alone."

Then the Ford jolted out of the cover of scrub cedar and juniper, and blue jays rose scolding. It was just as the Navajo had said. The building was burned to the ground. Only a few large beams still smoldered, and a stack of what had been sacked piñon nuts was a mass of hot coals. They searched first back of the store where Frank's bedroom had been, poking among ruins too hot to touch. They feared to find charred bones. They found nothing; not even melted silver. Robbery, then.

Once they turned to the hay barn, about fifty feet from the house, which the fire had not reached. It was locked, but peering through a small dusty window the men could see that it was full of baled hay. Mahan noticed that above the hay, directly in front of the door, something stuck up like a saddle horn.

"A saddle," he reported, "probably in pawn. The fellow must have come on a horse or he'd have taken the saddle."

When Sam Day drove up with a Navajo policeman they had nothing to report, but went over the ground again. When they came to the locked barn, after hours of hopeless search, Sabin called out in a choked voice. He was pointing to spots of blood on the snow and on a heavy wagon reach that lay behind a wood pile.

"It'll be inside," he said with conviction. "We'll find poor Frank inside. They expected the barn to catch fire, and it didn't. Bring me that reach — help me here!"

Using the heavy pole as a battering ram, four men ran against the door until the lock broke, the door swung open, and the body — frozen stiff — toppled out too quickly for them to catch it. That saddle horn, sticking up above the hay, was a human foot. Wedged in between the hay and the door, the body had been standing on its head which was beaten out of all human shape.

Reluctant with horror and grief, the men forced themselves to handle the body, examine it. They had all been fond of Frank, and they sickened at what they saw. He had been hit on the left side of the head repeatedly. Obviously, the wagon reach was the weapon used.

"Looks like a left-handed Indian did the job," said Day.

And Mahan, "And he hit from behind. The dirty skunk asked for hay and, when Frank was unlocking the door, he hit from behind. The dirty skunk!"

"And strong," said Sabin, more quietly. "Only a pretty strong man could wield that reach with such force."

Nothing more could be done there, so they sadly loaded the body into their car and drove back to St. Michaels. The next morning an inquest was held which resulted in the verdict "murder by parties unknown." It was not so stated, but most people agreed that those unknown parties were Navajos. The murder had all the earmarks of a Navajo killing.

In Gallup, the news stirred the town. Frank Dugan had been well liked. Mr. Manning had wired for Frank's brother, Pat, then warden of the state penitentiary in Santa Fe. Angry men met him, offering to "do the rest" if Frank's murderer was brought in. Pat Dugan's reply was characteristic. "I've been a peace officer too long," he said.

He drove out to St. Michaels where Sam Day had rounded up all the Navajos within fifteen miles. An all-night grilling had produced nothing. Neither had Marshal Day's careful examination of the ground. He showed Dugan; the ground was too hard for footprints. The killer would have to be tracked by his plunder. It should not be too hard to locate nine hundred pounds of flour and twelve hundred pounds of sugar. Trailing the jewelry — Mr. Manning had estimated that over a thousand dollars' worth had been taken — would be harder. Navajo thieves do not leave the reservation. Navajos say they bury their loot and leave it "until the sand is smooth again," until the case is forgotten. But cases are not forgotten.

Every trader on the reservation is on the lookout for easily identified pieces of jewelry. In handmade silver no absolute duplicates are possible; turquoise and shell wampum, more valued by the Navajo, are even easier to spot. It was only a matter of time until the killer would offer for sale a squash-blossom necklace or a string of wampum that was as good as a noose for his own neck.

As they talked, a government car drove up and Peter Parquette got slowly out. Looking straight at Sam Day, he addressed Pat Dugan. "Mr. Dugan," he said, "as Indian Agent I have come to take over. An investigator will be here from Washington. This is a case for the Indian Service; not for the US Marshal." Dark, heavy and stern, Parquette towered above the slighter man. Day set his jaw and his pale eyes flashed, but he turned away. Dugan merely nodded. State law does not run on Indian reservations; he had come as the victim's brother, not as a police officer.

Back in Gallup, Pat Dugan — still a brother, not an officer — listened to all who would talk. All agreed that there was bitter enmity between Parquette and Day who had clashed a time or two in court. Parquette was part Winnebago Indian; Sam Day's wife was Navajo. Both men had something of the secretiveness, the stealthiness of Indians. Each had many friends both Indians and white men. Both also had enemies who now recalled many charges, even a few indictments and judgments, involving such matters as selling sheep without permit and mishandling funds. Even Dugan and Parquette had met in court. Altogether it seemed to Pat Dugan, grieving for his young brother, that the effort to find Frank's murderer was getting lost among the local enmities. He stayed only for Frank's funeral and set out sadly for Santa Fe.

"It's too involved," he told Mr. Manning at the train, "for a simple officer of the law."

The case was indeed involved. Navajos live a complicated life of their own, mostly hidden from whites, touching the white man's culture only through schools, agencies, and the trader. Nobody is more important than the trader. He is first a storekeeper, operating under federal license. He carries flour, bacon, canned goods, and candy; calico, velvet, tobacco, medicines, shawls, shovels, and shirts. He is also a banker and makes loans, taking as security the silver, turquoise, and wampum that are the Navajo's capital, as well as his adornment. Under the law, the trader must lend without interest, and loans must run a year. After that the trader does as he likes. Some are good collectors, many let loans run indefinitely and even allow trustworthy Navajos to borrow their own jewelry for the great tribal ceremonies. Navajos know where the fine pieces are — what is redeemed, what is still in pawn.

Sam Day, knowing Navajos and having his own ideas, continued to look around. At Cross Canyon he had learned that Yellow Policeman had a lot of flour and sugar, and a wampum necklace with two bracelets tied to it that had been in pawn at the Cross Canyon store. It was a tip worth investigating. He decided to go to Kle-ge-toh Wash and call on Yellow Policeman whom he knew well as an influential Navajo, headman of his district and a Navajo policeman. In spite of his government job, Yellow Policeman was known to have little use for whites; scorning white ways, he continued to live as an old Navajo with several wives. Any crime Yellow Policeman was connected with might have a sexual as well as a financial basis.

Despite the vast distances that separate them, reservation dwellers, both white and red, lead lives that are far from dull. The stoic manner and impassive faces often conceal high romance and vicious hatreds, spiced by sardonic humor and fed by malicious gossip. Many traders have married Navajo girls, considered highly seductive; many live with them unwed. Navajos consider this the girl's own business, though it may reduce her value in the matrimonial market. As late as 1922, wives were openly bought. Even in the case of an irregular association, if it became permanent the man was supposed to pay. A white man who did not pay or who played "the coyote," taking another man's wife, might find himself some dark night lying among the embers of his store with a broken head.

None of this applied to Frank Dugan, but Sam Day had heard Navajos complain that he was a hard collector. Navajos have not known money long, but they love it, are sharp traders, inveterate gamblers, and capable of long resentment and savage reprisal. He thought of this as his Ford straddled the high centers, rushed the sandy hills, and generally acted as though it had been built for the reservation.

Yellow Policeman's establishment was typical of the rich Navajo's home. An old woman was stirring a pot on a low fire outside the largest hogan. Children and dogs played under the piñon trees. Under a large, gnarled cedar sat a young woman weaving a blanket. Sonne, the favorite wife. She was a charmer with smooth skin, delicate features, long hair, and well-marked brows over almond eyes.

122

Yellow Policeman was not at home, but lounging there were three other men Day was glad to see. As a member of the tribe and with complete knowledge of the language, he had heard gossip that linked them with Yellow Policeman; perhaps with the crime at Cross Canyon. He knew their Navajo names, but as an officer he used their white ones: Doc, John Billy, and John King. Undaunted by their typical refusal to answer questions, Sam Day kept on probing. In time they emitted enough gutterals to state that Yellow Policeman had got flour and sugar from Hubbell's, on credit. This was easy to verify and proved true.

Doc, naming nobody, said: "Sometimes you don't like people bad enough to kill."

John Billy, also without mentioning a name, remembered that somebody had lain, for many nights, on the cliffs above Cross Canyon.

Then Yellow Policeman rode up. A boy took over his gaunt roan, and the headman strode toward the group. Over six feet tall, he had a firm jaw, cruel eyes, small mustache, and the yellowish skin that gave him his name. He greeted Day in Navajo. The conversation was long, strung out by silences. At last, long last, Yellow Policeman admitted that he had got the wampum and bracelets from Hosteen Begay. (This name means "Son of a Man" and serves as would John Doe in English.)

Sam Day knew that young man well. Under twenty, he was slim and beautiful. He moved with the Navajo's feline grace, but his soft brown eyes and fine sallow skin indicated white blood, reputed to come from one of the best families in the Southwest. Hosteen Begay was in love with Sonne, as the reservation gossips well knew. Likely he had given her the bracelets. Day, following Navajo custom, limited his talk to men, but he watched Sonne demurely weaving. She fitted the tale well. Nobody knew where her suitor was. Just before dark Day left. The guilty, he felt sure, were there.

Later, three young Navajos told Day that they had met Begay the afternoon before the killing, fourteen miles from Cross Canyon. Yes, he was mounted and his deerskin saddle bags bulged. No, they did not know where he was going. A mounted man could, of course, have ridden those fourteen miles before night. But Sam Day, for reasons unstated, dropped the matter of Hosteen Begay. Two days later he arrested Yellow Policeman, Doc, John Billy and John King. In Gallup he formally charged them with the murder of Frank Dugan.

Everybody on the reservation now took sides. Sam Day, believing in the guilt of Yellow Policeman and his friends, was doing all he could to befriend Hosteen Begay. Parquette and his party thought the boy had been an accomplice or a tool, if not solely guilty of the crime. He believed in the innocence of Yellow Policeman and his friends and was supported by Chee Dodge, the most influential Navajo with both whites and Indians. Yellow Policeman, he claimed, was not a man to commit murder. He employed Frank Walker, a halfbreed, to seek more evidence. Some people said, and still say, that the murder was planned, if not actually committed, by a white man. Certain white men were named, even left-handed men who might have fitted that description of the killer, but nothing was ever brought out in court.

Parquette had reported to Washington and the Department of Justice had sent out a man named White as investigator. He heard

124

all the gossip and recriminations, made no comment, and followed his own lines.

Here the affair rested for almost a year. Frank Walker was listening here and there. Hosteen Begay was not molested. Yellow Policeman and his associates waited, confident they would not be brought to trial. As, in fact, they never were. And Mr. White kept on driving from one trading post to another picking up pawn from Cross Canyon. The same Indian was named in every deal, but Mr. White evidently thought his case was not complete.

Then one day two Navajo boys rode into the agency at Ft. Defiance and asked to see Mr. Parquette. One of them was Hosteen Begay; the other a friend whose name was never linked with the crime. What happened in that interview nobody knows. Sam Day first heard of it when Jim Morgan, Begay's Navajo half-brother, rode up to his place in St. Michaels and reported that Begay had confessed the murder of Frank Dugan.

Jim was distracted. "The boy should have come to me first," he moaned. "I told him he's as good as hanged now. Parquette is against him, and he can never overcome those who will use him to save themselves."

No reason appears for Hosteen Begay's sudden confession. Nobody was after him just then. Sam Day, taking the romantic slant, thought the lad was desperate because a girl he loved would not have him — not Sonne; by this time it was another girl. Versatile chaps, these Navajos.

Others maintained that Begay came to Ft. Defiance with no idea of confessing and was tortured into admitting the crime, but that he sturdily refused to implicate others. Mr. Day believed that his confession did implicate others and was therefore suppressed. Certainly no written confession appears in the record. Nor has it ever been explained why Hosteen Begay, a confessed murderer, was allowed the run of the place. Had he bought himself off by protecting someone else? Answers to these and other questions crop up all over the reservation, but the answers contradict each other too flatly and incriminate too many men to be quoted.

It may be stated that Begay, left unguarded at Ft. Defiance, stole a horse and ran away. If he had taken to the north country then, he might have lived out his life in peace and quiet. But he went to Kle-ge-toh Wash, where Yellow Policeman lived. Sam Day says that he was going to see Sonne, who had promised to tell the truth if he did. Mr. Day believed until he died that Sonne knew how the crime was committed, where the loot was cached. But, apparently, Sonne refused to talk. Her affair with Begay was over by then; she refused to incriminate her husband. It was the fugitive's only chance.

Yellow Policeman owed him wages, so Begay took what seemed a fair equivalent: a horse and a gun.

Thus equipped, Hosteen Begay took refuge in the wilderness, broken country where the only growth was piñon, cedar, and sage; and waterholes were ten miles apart. There he could live on what he killed — as long as his ammunition held out. He was now a menace to Yellow Policeman, as well as an outlaw. Parquette issued orders that he should be taken, dead or alive: a strange order from a man who had been so lax in guarding the prisoner. If Begay had been killed then, the case might have been dropped, but the Navajos seemed afraid of him. Once, while he slept, somebody stole his horse and gun but did not disturb him. That left him with only a hammerless .38 pistol and a small supply of ammunition. About two weeks after this, Begay went back to Kle-ge-toh Wash, presumably to appeal again to Sonne.

A wash is a sandy riverbed, dry most of the year, with steep banks cut down by the raging torrents of the rainy season. Near Kle-ge-toh were three huts: one empty, one where Yellow Policeman lived, one occupied by his blind father. Hosteen Begay went into the blind man's hogan and took bread and meat. Then he slipped into the empty hogan, ate his food, and waited for a chance to see Sonne. As he lay there, men came up outside and talked.

Begay recognized Yellow Policeman and John King; the others might have been Doc and John Billy. He heard them say that they would kill him if they found him. They talked a long time. Begay, weary and weak from many days with little food, fell asleep. When he woke it was broad day, and the men had discovered his hide-out.

Hosteen Begay's reputation as a dangerous man probably saved him from a rush. Nobody approached him, except John King who swarmed up the side of the hogan and called down taunts through the smoke vent.

"Tonight," he prophesied, "you'll eat with your grandmother!" Both Begay's grandmothers had gone to their rewards: the known Navajo grandmother, and the stately white dame gossips had granted him.

As the day advanced, more and more Navajos came, called by their mysterious under-ground. By night two hundred men were there, all afraid to face one desperate boy crouching in a hogan. At last a woman went in, Yellow Policeman's sister.

"What are you afraid of?" she asked, and walked in.

Begay, scorning to touch a woman, stepped to the door, armed only with his hammerless pistol. "Where is John King?" he called

John King, less brash now than when he called down the smoke hole, was behind a piñon tree. The other two hundred found other trees: a perfect example of the Indian's way of fighting by disappearing. Only Yellow Policeman's brother, yelling for his gun, rode full tilt onto Begay who side-stepped the horse and shot, creasing the man under the chin. A second shot grazed his hand. Doc, by that time, was running his pony up the wash. Begay shot again, but missed. When he tried again his gun jammed, but nobody interfered as he ran up the draw into the straggling woods.

There he tried to break his gun down to reload. As he knelt, a boy rode toward him. He had come to offer help, but Begay was too excited to recognize a friend. He tried the gun again, aiming at the boy. This time it fired, but slipped and wounded his own foot. Reloading, limping, in pain, he ran back toward the hogans, cut a horse loose from a team and mounted. Just then Yellow Policeman's brother fired, and the shot went through Hosteen Begay just under the heart. A fraction of an inch higher and it would have killed him. As it was, he was only losing more blood. Desperate, he wheeled his horse and rode directly at the armed man who shot again, and missed. Two men on the hill shot, and missed. Begay dashed down the draw after Yellow Policeman's brother. As he went, the boy who had brought the rifle crossed his trail. Begay shot at him, but the shot went wild. Then he turned and circled the little settlement again; the third time.

Hosteen Begay was riding like a crazy man, weak from loss

of blood, and his gun was empty. As he rode, he broke it down to reload and the cylinder flipped out. Now he had no weapon; only a very potent reputation as a dangerous man. Then he fainted and slipped from his horse; the Indians were afraid to approach him. Nobody knows how long he lay there. When he came to he was suffering, weak, unarmed, unhorsed, but still plucky. The white man who had fathered that boy might have been proud to own him. Sam Day, who told this story, said he had never been able to decide whether Hosteen Begay was the bravest man he ever knew, or the craziest.

Still hopeful, it seems, that Sonne might incriminate her husband, Begay ran toward Yellow Policeman's hogan, opening his pocket-knife. Sonne cowered inside with her mother-in-law, an eighteen-year-old boy, and a child. The boy had an ax. Warding off his blow, Begay gave him an upper-cut on the chin. One of the women snatched the boy's ax, the other held Begay until Yellow Policeman's brother dashed in and threw him. Then all the others, courageous once more, swarmed in.

Only one came to the rescue. He pulled the other man off, talked reason, and sent for the nearest white man, George Mahan, now managing the rebuilt Cross Canyon store. The Indians made no objection as Mahan moved the wounded Begay to the hospital at Ft. Defiance.

A warrant was issued against Hosteen Begay for the murder of Frank Dugan, and he was turned over to Sam Day, as Deputy Marshal. Even then, Mr. White, the agent of the Department of Justice, held no formal investigation, though his collection of jewelry picked up in many posts all came from the Cross Canyon store, by way of Hosteen Begay. Possibly he, too, thought that others besides the twenty-year-old boy were guilty, and hoped for evidence against them as well.

For two years longer nothing was done. Day could not persuade anyone to follow up the evidence he had collected against Yellow Policeman, Doc, John King, and John Billy. White went on driving around over the reservation. Parquette kept his own counsel. And Begay, that genius with the ladies, got involved with yet another one. He wanted to marry her, but was not considered eligible with the murder charge pending. Again, he was unguarded at Ft. Defiance; but he made no attempt to escape. One season in the wilderness had satisfied him.

Then one night, Claude Romero's trading post at Kinna Zinna was robbed. Pendleton blankets were taken, and some jewelry. A well-marked trail through the timber led unmistakably to Hosteen Begay. Sam Day was under the unhappy necessity of again arresting the boy he had tried so hard to save. It was inevitable that the murder charge should be renewed. Mr. White, who was certainly free of local enmities, saw no reason now for delay and Hosteen Begay was brought to trial in 1925 for the murder of Frank Dugan in 1922.

As the Cross Canyon store was in Arizona, the trial took place in Phoenix. Begay, defended by a lawyer appointed by the court, pleaded guilty. He told how he had worked for Dugan in order to study his habits, how he had asked for hay when Dugan was alone, how he had struck to kill. His story did not implicate anyone else. Sam Day, romantic to the end, said that Begay had given up hope of his lady-love — not Sonne, nor the second, but another one — and was ready to die. Nobody knows why, after his apparent desperate efforts to implicate Yellow Policeman and the others, he stood alone at the last. Nobody understands a Navajo, anyhow.

The trial was brief. It is generally thought that Hosteen Begay's white father used his influence to get a sentence of life imprisonment instead of death. Since then he has been paroled and is again on the reservation, living a life of usefulness. Hence he figures in this story not under his own name but under one that means no more than John Doe.

7. The Manby Mystery

On Wednesday, the third of July, 1929, life in Taos seemed to be rocking along in its usual peaceful rut. The American Legion and the Taos Pueblo teams were getting ready for their annual baseball game on the Fourth. Artists were painting in their cool adobe studios. Indian men rode into town on runty ponies and women walked behind them with the spreading gait of wide-topped buckskin boots. The plaza was filled with shoppers: artist's wives with bulging string bags, family swarms jabbering in Spanish, Mormons in from ranches, tourists buying postcards and gas. A United States Deputy Marshal drove bumpily up the narrow mountain road from Santa Fe.

He came to serve papers on Arthur Manby in renewal of an old suit. Seven years before, a woman had followed up a visit to Taos by suing Manby for breach of promise, and won judgment for $14,000. As Manby owned no property in his own name, this claim had never been paid, and would expire unless the suit was reopened. The officer found Manby's house locked. Neighbors, knowing his errand, suggested that the old man was hiding out. The deputy was persistent. He came several times in the course of the day and finally, as he knocked at doors and windows, he saw something that aroused his suspicions. He called a deputy sheriff. The local officer also peered through a window and became alarmed. Neighbors were summoned.

What they saw was a thick swarm of flies, clinging to a screen door and buzzing madly.

Unable to break any of the heavy doors, the men climbed up onto the flat roof and looked over into the patio. There they saw four raging dogs, foaming and snarling, maddened probably by thirst. Their pans were empty; they could not reach the water in the well. The officers shot the dogs, dropped into the patio, slit the screen, opened the latch, and entered a narrow passage. At first their attention was occupied by the police dog which had been Manby's constant companion. He also showed evidence of madness, so they shot him. Then they came upon the body, lying on an army cot.

As though the man had thrown himself down to rest, the body lay easily on its side, partly covered with a blanket, one hand hanging, and showing no evidence of violence — none, that is, except that the head was gone, severed at the collar bone. The body was dressed in underwear and a sweater. Shoes, socks, riding breeches, and puttees lay dropped carelessly on the floor. Keys attached to a

134

long chain were fastened to the trousers. The condition of the body was too revolting for description; it must have lain there for several hot days. In the adjoining room they found a human skull, yellowed and stripped clean as though the dog had worried it for many hours.

The five men agreed that the body was Manby's. They testified later that the idea of murder did not occur to them. They thought the old man had died in the night and that the dog, maddened by the smell of death, had gnawed off his head. Everything called for haste, so a coroner's jury was summoned at once. Their report stated that "nothing was found to indicate that death was due to other than natural causes." They issued a burial permit, and the body and the skull were buried in the garden. Manby was not a member of a church, he had no plot in the cemetery, and he was buried in a spot he had once mentioned as suitable.

Taos was agog with excitement. It was the most thrilling Fourth of July in years. Nobody had liked Manby, so there were few regrets; only wild theories as to the cause of his death, chuckling guesses as to which of his lady friends would inherit, and the telling and retelling of every known fact of the old man's life.

"Old Man Manby" was a queer figure even in Taos, where pig-tailed Indians swathe themselves in sheets, artist men and women dress indistinguishably, and tourists present the oddest figures of all. Among them, Manby made a daily appearance, plodding into Burch's store for groceries or to the post office. He wore corduroy riding breeches, boots, and a dilapidated hat — all dirty. He carried a revolver in its holster and a police dog walked at his heels. Often he rode a slow horse out to Teresita's tourist camp. He visited nobody else and few people passed through the high adobe wall that hid his house from Pueblo Road. Inside, the house faced a pleasant formal garden with rows of poplars and a lilac-bordered lawn for tea. It had been rented now and then to people who opened up its iron-barred windows, aired its heavy-walled rooms, and set potted plants in the sunroom. But as a rule, Manby lived there alone, not even admitting the Indian who occasionally flooded the garden from the ditch and hoed the weedy flower beds.

The known facts were few. Arthur Rockfort Manby was an Englishman, graduate of a good university, and assumed to be a remittance man: one of those scions of good family whose income depends upon their not going home. During his forty years in New Mexico, Arthur Manby had been involved in a multiplicity of schemes, many of them questionable. Tales were told of bizarre mining ventures, of advance payments accepted for land to which Manby could show no clear title. He had often been in court, both as plaintiff and defendant, and more than once he lost because it was proved that he had been unethical. Gossips said that Manby was a miser with immense sums of money hidden in his house. Gossips also built fantastic tales on his daily visits to Teresita Ferguson who ran a tourist camp, and with whom it was thought he had business dealings. Altogether a morose, secretive, grasping old man whom nobody liked.

The body and the head were buried on the third. On the fourth visitors swarmed into the Manby house. The deputy sheriff in charge, tolerant of a natural curiosity, acted as guide rather than guard. People went through all the rooms, monkeying with the chains and locks, tapping wainscotings and cupboard backs, making guesses as to where the treasure was buried. Some expected to find fruit jars filled with gold nuggets or gold washings. Nobody doubted that there was treasure, for Manby kept no bank account and his takings from recent sales must be in the house. But no money was found. Neither was there any evidence of theft, except that the old man's best suit of clothes was missing, and his one reputable hat.

Among the first visitors was a lady who passed Doc Martin's house with such determined mien that the Doctor removed his pipe to point to her.

"Looks like she knew her way, hey?" he commented to the butcher who shared his bench.

The lady had precipitated a recent excitement when she dashed out of her chile joint, screaming that her diamonds had been stolen. The town was more interested in where she got her diamonds than in who had stolen them, for her impulsive announcement seemed to confirm certain suspicions which the butcher had summed up at the time.

"Like as not the old coot found it handier to give her the family jewels than cash. And he's just took 'em back again."

The lady may have reached the same conclusions, for she made no formal charges, and her little whirlwind soared off into indifference. Now she was important again as one, at least, of several possible heiresses. Setting her small feet in mincing steps that swung her pillowy rear, she pushed through the crowded hall and into one of the bedrooms. As she met other mourners, she dropped appropriate remarks.

"Sad, so sad! My poor old friend. A fine man. Sad, how sad!"

In the bedroom she encountered the deputy, telling again about the flies on the screen, how he had climbed over the roof, how bravely he had dropped into the patio, how he had forced the door. As the lady listened, standing near the head of the bed, she ran her hand under the mattress — a most natural gesture. The deputy had hardly got beyond "opening the door" in his tale when a scream spoiled his climax. The lady was swinging a small chamois bag over her head.

"My diamonds," she squalled, "my diamonds!"

When the butcher and the Doctor met on the plaza the next day, the butcher told the story.

"Sure they let her take 'em," he said. "The old buzzard probably gave 'em to her. I don't doubt she earned 'em."

Amid all this drama and excitement everybody neglected to notify the District Attorney, Fred Stringfellow. He lived in Raton a hundred miles across the mountains and he learned of Manby's death only when another case took him to Taos on July 5th. Mr. Stringfellow at once introduced some dignity into the proceedings. First he learned who had seen Manby last. One recent visitor was a woman who had gone through the house in late June with the idea of renting it.

"Though my call was unexpected," she said, "Mr. Manby greeted me courteously at the side door, patting his growling dog; but I thought that huge police dog kept a hostile eye on me all the time. I entered a narrow hallway with an unmade army cot in the corner. The facing door into the patio was fastened with a heavy iron bar. We went on into the dining room where unwashed dishes stood among dusty papers on the table, and rancid butter melted on a plate. A rolltop desk was almost buried under red-taped documents, filing boxes, and long yellowing newspaper clippings. And incongruously on the wall hung a series of delicate watercolors — garden scenes, Venetian canals, and ferny dells — done by Manby himself years ago as a student in Vienna.

138

"'Nobody knows,' the old man gloated, 'how much I have controlled from that desk.' Maybe I could have got the whole story then, but he had a distressing habit of putting his face close, the room stank of an oil stove and of dogs. I did not encourage my host to talk, but he rambled on.

"'President Roosevelt,' I remember his saying, 'was in constant touch with me; I have dozens of letters which show his confidence in my plans . . . No revolution has occurred in Mexico in the last twenty-five years which was not planned right here . . . I could show you papers! . . . Those men in Cimarron and Raton are a bunch of skunks . . . So far they have won in the venal courts, but some day you will see . . . Unless they get me first . . . they are after me, and sooner or later they'll get me . . .'

"His talk was like that: defiant confidence in what he could do, and then sudden lapses into quavering fear. All the bravery was in his talk; his living arrangements showed only fear. We went through the kitchen, which was obviously unused, and into a scullery beyond. I approached the door into the patio where four powerful police dogs paced restlessly. Manby stopped me.

"'Don't think of trying to enter the patio,' he said. 'I can save you from this dog in here; he is trained not to molest my friends. But those would tear anybody except me to pieces. They are my best protection.' I noticed then that he wore his gun even in his own house.

"We went back through the dining room and hall and a long series of rooms, all opening onto three patios. Every room had barred windows, many with heavy wooden shutters also barred. The wide front entrance opening from the garden to the front patio had been divided by a rough board partition with a locked door.

139

The big front door was chained and bolted, as was every door. Manby opened each one with keys from a big bunch he carried on a chain. The rooms were furnished with heavy pieces, some of them very fine, and in every room was a dirty unkempt bed.

" 'You see, I sleep in a different bed every night. They'll get me some day, but I'm putting it off as long as I can.'

"It was too unpleasant to linger over. I admired the garden which he spoke of as one of his many efforts to create civilized living in this barbaric land, and found myself with relief in the sunny and friendly street."

Manby's last known visitors were two young artists who had called on him on Sunday morning, June 30. He acted queerly; not drunk, they thought, but possibly doped. He complained that his enemies had been blowing poison gas in over the wall that separated his patio from his neighbor's. The young painters assumed, as everyone did, that the old man was lightly touched in the head, made no careful inquiries, and soon went away.

A maid at Teresita's tourist camp testified that on that Sunday afternoon she had overheard a bitter quarrel between Manby, Teresita Ferguson, and young Carmel Duran. Duran was presumed to be Manby's rival. The quarrel seemed to hinge on Manby's request that Teresita should come to live with him and take care of him. Both Teresita and Duran testified that they had not seen Manby since. Neither had anyone else. That was probably the day of the old man's death — by natural causes, by a maddened dog, or by an unknown killer.

This Teresita was the daughter of a Scotch miner, Jack Ferguson. She had once been married but was the mother of several children born since her separation from her husband. Among Manby's

140

papers were found many references to her as his business partner and as his "Princess Teresita." As his business partner, Teresita now held the controlling interest in the Colonial Bond and Security Company, which Manby had controlled. What money he had seemed to be there. As heiress, Teresita moved into Manby's house, took possession of his personal property, and auctioned off what she did not move to her own house.

Mr. Stringfellow, hoping for a clue, set about collecting facts that might show a motive for the old man's killing. He at once found himself dealing with old folklore, gossip, and unprovable speculation. Every line of inquiry seemed to lead to Teresita Ferguson and her affairs. The facts, as nearly as they have been established, were these.

Years before, Jack Ferguson, in partnership with one "Shorty" Wilkerson, a prospector, and Clarence Probert of Taos, had owned the Mystic Mine in the mountains above Taos. Adjoining the Mystic was the Aztec Mine, owned by wealthy and respected citizens of the neighboring county of Colfax. For years there had been bad feeling between the owners of the two mines. Ferguson, Wilkerson, and Probert accused the Aztec owners of trespass; the Aztec owners accused Ferguson and Wilkerson of high-grading — that is, in plain words, of stealing ore from the Aztec Mine. At various times the owners of the Aztec tried to buy the Mystic, but unsuccessfully. It was said that Wilkerson refused to sell.

During the winter of 1920-21, Wilkerson disappeared. The story told by his partners, Ferguson and Probert, was that they had found his body in the Mystic Mine, killed by a gun shot and headless. They said they buried the body, though they could not find the head. They told that Wilkerson had that day met with the owners of the Aztec, and they voiced dire suspicions. Suspicious or not, they stopped for a meal at the Aztec Mine. On their way home both men became violently sick; both were in bed for weeks. The owners of the Aztec Mine said they had not seen Wilkerson; they did not believe that Ferguson and Probert had found a body or buried it, though they thought a skeleton found years later might have been Wilkerson's. None of this ever came to court.

Ferguson was left with a malady which seemed to affect his mind. For several years he lived in his daughter's tourist camp, a dotty old man. All day, the neighbors reported, he sat in the sun, saying little but growing more haggard and wild-eyed as the months passed. And at night they often heard screams. His hoarse, pitiful cries were mostly unintelligible, but sometimes words could be distinguished. They had to do with heads floating in the air. Often he shouted: "Wilkerson, take your head, take it away!" Gossips stated later that somebody had scared the old man into insanity with sheeted ghosts and faked bodiless heads. All this became too upsetting to the tourist business, and Ferguson was placed in the state insane asylum. After a few months he was discharged as cured. Quieter then, he lived five or six years longer, a weakened, frightened old man, and his daughter took charge of his affairs.

Mr. Stringfellow then called on George Downer, an Albuquerque attorney who had been retained by Teresita Ferguson in the winter of 1926-27. She had engaged Mr. Downer to get an accounting from Alvin Burch of Taos for a trust fund of $827,000,000. *Eight hundred twenty-seven million dollars!* This amount was so fantastic that Mr. Downer's first impulse was to refuse the case. But he was tempted by the very idiocy of the claim. Perhaps, he thought, getting certain people on the witness stand might uncover interesting facts about the high-grading and the unexplained death of Wilkerson. Probably enough money was involved to be worth a lot of trouble to somebody. But as he studied the case, Mr. Downer found not clarification, but only greater confusion.

Teresita, middle-aged, heavyset, with a cool green eye and an assured manner, was articulate enough as far as she went, but vague just when hard facts were most needed. She said that during her father's illness his brother from Kansas had engaged detectives to investigate Wilkerson's death. She hinted that she thought Wilkerson's murder and the poisoning of her father and Probert were part of a plot to acquire the Mystic Mine. She would not say whom she suspected.

Teresita could remember the name of only one of the detectives, a Severino Gutierrez who, she said, came from Washington, and who represented the "United States Secret and Civil Service, Self-Supporting Branch." This gentleman had offered proof, convincing to Teresita, that certain important men were responsible for the death of Wilkerson and the subsequent poisoning of Ferguson and Probert. Mr. Gutierrez had evidence so convincing, she said, that the guilty had settled with her through Mr. Gutierrez for the amazing sum of $827,000,000.

No, Teresita had not received a check; only a "certificate" made out to her for this sum. She said she had signed the certificate in two or three places and given it to her old friend, Alvin Burch, as trustee to deposit in a bank in Denver. In due time Mr. Burch returned from Denver and stated that he had deposited the certificate. Teresita saw no receipt or record of deposit. That was in October, 1926. A few weeks later the invaluable Mr. Gutierrez, she said, had deposited to the same account the sum of $200,000. This was in the form of "free gold," and Mr. Downer thought he was nearing the center of the mystery. Free gold is what would be acquired by high-grading. In January, 1927, Jack Ferguson died and Teresita became the owner of the Mystic Mine.

Since then, Teresita told her attorney, Alvin Burch had steadily refused to give her an accounting of his trusteeship of her millions. Mr. Downer, highly skeptical, wrote Mr. Burch a formal demand for an accounting, and set out to try to establish a few sane facts. He wished first to know who Mr. Gutierrez was; and then how much money, if any, was actually involved..

The owners of the Aztec Mine denied any business dealings with Teresita Ferguson; they had never seen, dealt with, or even heard of her agent, Severino Gutierrez. Mr. Gutierrez was proving to be an elusive, though potent force.

Up to this time, Arthur Manby had not appeared in Teresita's consultations with her attorney, though their association was in full flower and seemed to involve business as well as sentimental relations. But Teresita asked Mr. Downer to send Mr. Manby a copy of his letter to Alvin Burch, and Mr. Manby now took over as Teresita's nearest friend. He wrote Mr. Downer many long and involved letters which might indicate a disordered mind, but which showed a shrewd grasp of money matters. Mr. Manby strongly advised that all investigation of the trust fund be dropped forthwith. He gave his opinion that Alvin Burch was a crook. This judgment was not confirmed by anybody in Taos where Alvin Burch was well known as an honest and trustworthy citizen.

When questioned, Alvin Burch seemed frightened. He insisted that he knew nothing, that he had acted under orders, but he refused to name anybody. Finally he admitted that he had signed the agreement with Teresita and deposited the certificate. He would not name the amount of the trust fund, but under questioning he stated that the income from it had been invested in oil lands in Mexico; about $80,000. That amount, Mr. Downer calculated, would be the interest on a deposit of about a million dollars. Still too much money to make sense. And there was no record of any of these deposits.

Herbert Cheetham, a former government investigator, who was not employed on the case but who made some inquiries of his own, states that a sub-treasury official told him that the certificate Burch took to Denver was a counterfeit United States Treasury certificate. In Denver it was at once detected and confiscated. It was so poor a forgery that no charges were made.

Mr. Burch seemed especially nervous, reluctant, and frightened when questioned about the mythical Severino Gutierrez. He admitted that he had never actually seen the man, though he showed complete confidence that such a person existed and was the director of the "United States Civil and Secret Service, Self-Supporting Branch." Mr. Burch was a member of this chimerical organization, which other Taos people had belonged to. Mr. Manby told them that he was constantly receiving messages or "signs" from airplanes flying over, or from license plates on certain out-of-state automobiles he could point out. Some of his associates thought he kept carrier pigeons, and flew signals from his flagpole to his colleagues in the planes. Meetings were held in Mr. Manby's house and both Manby and Teresita were always present. Mr. Gutierrez came too, according to the members, arriving secretly in Taos by private plane from Washington. He never showed himself at meetings but spoke from behind a curtain. Generally, Mr. Gutierrez' orders came in the form of notes. Later, some of these notes came to light and were easily shown to be in Teresita's handwriting. Clumsy as was all this staging and sleight-of-hand, Manby and Teresita had raised several thousand dollars among trusting Taos folk; the Burch family alone had supported that "self-supporting branch" to the extent of some $17,000. None of the other contributing members came forward, nor were they ever summoned to court. They had all been taken in, of course, with the bait of wealth to come.

Here was a mass of fantastic nonsense, as absurd as a drunkard's dream, even sinister in its evidence of wrongdoing against simple and trusting people; but little that a sensible attorney could make stand up in court. Mr. Downer, nevertheless, was still hoping that when he got Manby on the witness stand he could establish facts about Teresita's wealth — perhaps even about "Shorty" Wilkerson's death. So he brought a civil suit for Teresita Ferguson against Alvin Burch, demanding an accounting. The hearing was set for the July session of court in 1929. When Arthur Manby was found dead and beheaded on July 3rd, the case was postponed and has never come to trial.

All this evidence was now for the District Attorney to mull over. So he did, but found nothing that led to Manby's death, nothing to justify the arrest of anybody for murder. A detective was engaged for a while, but Taos County had no funds for a vigorous investigation, and there was no public demand for it. People were entranced with the mystery, amused and amazed with Manby's financial and romantic doings, but not really concerned about his loss. In the town where he had lived for thirty years, Arthur Manby had no friends to demand a full investigation of his

146

death. Within a few weeks all official inquiry was dropped, and only gossip remained lively.

Manby's "Princess Teresita" had easily established her position as heiress through her interest in the Colonial Bond and Security Company which owned all of Manby's assets — his house, its contents, and a hot spring near Taos. The house was heavily mortgaged to a New York man. Efforts were made to sell it, but with no success. At last the mortgage was foreclosed and Teresita moved out. When the lawyer's fees were paid, Taos gossip estimated Manby's estate as worth *one two-dollar bill and one buffalo nickel.*

Meanwhile, Eardley B. Manby of Woodhall Spa, England and Fred V. Manby of Cluny, Canada had come forward. They were brothers of Arthur Manby and they were also financially interested in the Colonial Bond and Security Company. In a letter addressed to Governor Richard C. Dillon of New Mexico, these two gentlemen, "grieved and shocked," stated that they considered it the "duty of the state to investigate and bring the criminal to justice . . ." The letter continued: "The victim of this dreadful tragedy was a man of distinguished parts, and for over forty years he worked hard in developing the resources of Colfax and Taos Counties. His abilities were recognized by the leading statesmen of the United States, and he was a frequent correspondent of the late President Roosevelt, who recognized his ability in matters pertaining to the United States.

"Notwithstanding his devotion to the country of which he was a citizen, he was dumped into a box and buried in his own garden like a dog. I am sure you will agree that this is not the kind of treatment that should be meted out to a Christian anywhere in the world. The members of the family, therefore, look to the governor of New Mexico to make a thorough investigation of this cruel and brutal assassination. The victim's head was battered and severed from his body, and the verdict of the coroner's jury of natural causes was absolutely a false one.

"The members of his family resident in the United States, Canada, and England consider that the least the State of New Mexico can do is to give him a burial consistent and honorable."

Governor Dillon at once conferred with Mr. Stringfellow, attorney for the district including Taos, and Miguel A. Otero, Attorney General of New Mexico. This resulted in more investigations. The body was disinterred, the skull and viscera were sent to a laboratory for tests, many people were closely questioned. It was rumored that a detective had been retained. Any evidence uncovered obviously did not justify charging anybody with the murder of Manby, as no arrests were made. The public was left to satisfy its curiosity with the only official statement: the finding of the coroner's jury that Manby's death had resulted from natural causes.

Major Eardley Manby in England was not satisfied. He brought the matter to the attention of the British Foreign Office and hinted that the "member from Lincolnshire" might raise the matter in the House of Commons. Major Manby stated: "Apart from my brother's death, there is a mystery regarding what happened to the substantial property he possessed at the time of his death." But neither the House of Commons nor the British Foreign Office took action to revive the inquiry. Taos County could not, and the Manby family did not produce funds sufficient to engage a detective who might conceivably have unraveled the tangled web of Mr. Manby's affairs.

The questions that need answering are:

What was the purpose of that ridiculous secret society?

What was the purpose of that certificate of deposit?

Did Ferguson have a hoard of free gold? If so, where did he get it? and who got it at last?

What about the oil investment in Mexico?

There are no sensible answers. But there are five outstanding theories as to what happened to Manby:

First: that he was shot as he was getting ready for bed, the body arranged to look as though he had died naturally, and the head cut off and thrown to the dog.

Second: that Manby was killed elsewhere and his body carried to his house in the middle of the night.

Either of these theories presupposes a murderer who was known to the dogs. Neither offers any reasonable explanation for the ghoulish mutilation of the body.

Third: that Manby, who was ill, died quietly in his sleep, and the dog gnawed off his head.

Fourth: that Manby had a bleeding sore on his neck and that the dog, licking his master's wounds, might have been maddened by the taste of blood and killed and mutilated him.

Critics of these theories maintain that the dog could not have gnawed off the head without disturbing the body.

Fifth: that Manby, wishing to evade service of the papers in the breach of promise suit, and well-supplied with ready cash, left a body the size of his own, and disappeared.

This theory offers a reason for the removal of the head and also for the disappearance of Manby's one decent suit and hat. Its proponents say they have seen postcards from distant points, signed in Manby's handwriting. It is significant that Teresita has been the recipient of these cards.

Any of these solutions would probably please the mystery fan as being even more fantastic than the build-up. They will be disappointed by another solution though it accounts reasonably for all the facts. Those lost millions, that powerful secret society, those signs and portents, even the enigmatic Severino Gutierrez, were all the figments of an old man's diseased mind. The disease was a singularly loathesome one — paresis, which breaks down a mind into manias that vary from aggrandizement to persecution.

The only insoluble mystery about Mr. Manby's case is that anybody ever believed a word the old man said. Yet it is true that his crazy talk deluded worthy people, separated them from money, filled them with wild hopes and wilder fears. The people who were never under any delusions about the case were the physician, who knew the old man was a paretic, and the attorneys who studied the case. District Attorney Stringfellow and Judge Otero agreed that there was no evidence on which anybody could be charged with murder, no evidence indeed that murder had been done. All the evidence rather pointed to death from a typical case of general paresis.

Judge Otero and Mr. Stringfellow permit themselves to be quoted. Mr. Manby's physician identified the body, and his dentist the skull. That the maddened dog could have gnawed off the head is not unreasonable; other cases have been cited of police dogs who killed and gnawed at friendly people. Manby's dog had been locked into a hot house with neither food nor water for days. The condition of the body was such that close examination was impossible; nobody could say that the head had not been removed by a dog's sharp teeth.

But the crowning piece of evidence that proves the case not an unsolved murder, but a "death by natural causes," is Arthur Manby's diary. Among his papers were found two ordinary desk calendars covered with handwritten entries. They do not follow the dates; evidently the old man was using up paper he had. Many of the entries had been copied onto very thin paper bound into books kept in old-fashioned paper presses. These diaries cover two years. Students of psychopathology who have examined them say that they show typical paretic symptoms, especially aggrandizement and persecution mania. As his brain degenerated with disease, the old man actually believed that he was a powerful figure of international consequence, in touch with higher-ups too prominent to be named; that he controlled who-knows-what forces for good or evil; and that he was constantly menaced by enemies trying to kill him with poison gas or gunfire. In fact, the diaries prove that the most deluded of the old man's victims was Arthur Manby himself.

A late entry reflects clearly the old man's state of befuddlement, as well as its pitifulness. "T," (Teresita) he wrote, "cut loose on me, that I ought to have retired years ago as I was feeble, old, deaf, blind, etc. Some truth in that, as I told her, after being gassed and poisoned so often in her service and defense." After "blind, etc," the old man had added above a caret "and infected with disease." Apparently Manby understood his own condition.

The last entry is dated June 30, and reads: "Have been under the weather all week. Shortness of breath, no appetite, exhaustion following the least exercise. Probably result of last attempt to gas and poison me from T.P.'s side. Teresita denies this, but this does not change my belief."

June 30 was Sunday, the day the old man, weak and ill, called on Teresita and (according to the maid's testimony) begged her to come and take care of him. Doubtless he doddered weakly home after her refusal, and died alone.

8. Woo Dak San and the Bird

The morning of August 25, 1925 seemed much as usual in Silver City. Then D. B. Robertson, opening his plumbing shop on Bullard Street, missed his neighbor. Yee Fong was usually out by that time sweeping the sidewalk. Yee Fong ran a general store; but among the groceries were ingredients for Chinese dishes, among the dry-goods Chinese slippers and fans, and among the dishes bits of fine ware from China. Everybody liked the old man who had long ago cut off his pigtail, last link with China, and become a permanent and respected resident of the town. Always industrious and abstemious, they thought he must have thousands of dollars hid away somewhere; Yee Fong did not patronize the bank.

Mr. Robertson peeked through the crowded window. Nothing stirring within. Perhaps old Fong was sick. Mr. Robertson telephoned Joe Turner, the City Marshal, who left word at the sheriff's office. By the time Joe Turner had failed to get in the front door and gone round to the rear, Sheriff John Turner and Deputies Charlie Morrill and John St. John had come. They easily broke the flimsy lock and entered the back room. There they faced a seven-foot partition with a door, half open. Inside they saw Yee Fong. The body lay on its right side, head toward the door, stockinged feet toward the bed. There was a table, a trunk, an overturned chair. On the bed lay an ax, doubtless the weapon that had crushed the head. Blood had spattered the walls; on the floor was a red and sticky pool of it. Ordinary enough in the life of policemen. But what else they saw made them look at each other paling, gulping. Through Yee Fong's temple had been driven a butcher knife, a long murderous-looking instrument.

Sheriff Turner, protecting his hands with wrapping paper from a roll in the store, tried to pull out that knife. Tried, but could not. "Here," he grunted, "one of you fellows—" Only with Joe Turner's heavy foot on the head could the Sheriff, a tall stout man, pull the butcher knife free. It had gone clear through the head, pinning it to the floor. Mindful of finger prints, Sheriff Turner collected and carefully wrapped exhibits, and ordered his deputies to have the body removed and to pick up whom they could for questioning.

The officers searched for the thousands of dollars Yee Fong was supposed to have, but they found less than $700. Under a newspaper in the trunk tray was $600 in currency, $35 in gold and some small change in a money sack. Watch and chain had not been taken, but the officers accepted robbery as the motive. They smiled to find the small Chinese scales used for weighing opium. So the respectable Yee Fong was a hop merchant!

Pablo Benavides, twelve years old, said he had left the store the evening before about half past seven when he finished his work. Yee Fong was all right when he left. His brother Ramon, sixteen, testified that he was there later, playing cards with Yee as he often did. Yee Yik, a Chinese laundryman had been there in the evening, but had left early. The killing must have been late. There seemed to be nothing more to do. Sheriff Turner had planned a vacation and he left town, leaving Deputy Charles Morrill in charge of the office.

Silver City people thought they knew the Chinese. From earliest mining days the cook for the gang, the washee-washee, the owner of small store or restaurant, the house "boy" was familiar. With pigtail over his long cotton jacket, shuffling walk and folded hands, he was a well-behaved citizen, smilingly greeting friends, dependable in his dealings, reliable in paying his debts. But every one of these quiet friendly foreigners seemed to have another life hidden away behind the front where he worked. Perhaps it was a den of iniquity where opium was illegally dispensed or other Chinese were illegally held, after crossing the Rio Grande, until they could get along north and disappear into cities. Perhaps — but nobody thought much of this — the hidden life was only a Chinese nightingale, "with bright-bronze breast and bronze-brown wing," singing in Vachel Lindsay's poem of a lovely land where "spring came on forever."

It was Thursday when they found Yee Fong's body. On Sunday Deputies Morrill and St. John were driving along Broadway when a Chinese stepped out into the street to stop them.

"You know Woo Dak San" he asked. "Cook American Kitchen? He kill Yee Fong. Hop head hunting dope. This morning he left early for El Paso."

Without waiting for more the two deputies headed for the telephone. "Isn't that Woo Dak San the chink called Woo Foo who wanted us to help him collect back wages from that American Kitchen?"

"Sure thing! And he said he and other China boys were going to open that restaurant again."

Charlie Morrill talked with the police in El Paso. Woo Dak would have gone by stage to Deming and from there by train. He would have left Deming now. Maybe there would be time to catch him leaving the train at El Paso.

There was, just. Charles Mitchell picked up Woo Dak easily enough, sauntering through the station. At headquarters, they found $300 in each shoe, $80 in gold wrapped in tissue paper and stuck into his pocket. It was his, Woo Dak said; he would say nothing more. But on the way back to Silver City with Charlie Morrill, Woo Dak talked quite a lot. He had had dealings with Yee, he said; Yee sold dope, Woo Dak was an addict, he needed some right now. The El Paso police had given him a little, he said, "just so I quit crying and go to sleep." In Deming Deputy Morrill reported to the US narcotic officer that there was dope selling in Silver City. They had to stay over a night in Deming because the rainy season cloudbursts had brought the arroyos up. By that time Woo Dak was greenish in the face and shaking with his need for the drug. The narcotics man sympathetically gave him a small supply from his confiscated stock. Deputy Morrill was finding his prisoner tractable, pleasant, ready to talk, and interesting.

156

"How come you've got two names? They call you Woo Dak and Woo Foo."

"In China parents give a baby name; then he take another name himself so devil can't find him." Woo giggled. "Of course I don't believe that superstition. No, I didn't come from China first. I'm American citizen, born in Honolulu. I only went to China. Marry there . . . No, couldn't bring my wife back account the American laws. No Chinese wife can come in . . . My daughter nine years old now."

He would not admit knowing anything about the crime, but he did explain its oddity. "Chinese believe that if you cut optic nerve dead man can't see who killed him; can't come back. Chinese superstition. I don't believe that."

Back in Silver City, Deputy Morrill learned that the Chinese who had tipped them off to Woo Dak had left town, disappeared. He here leaves the tale, was never seen again; apparently no search was made for him. Woo Dak they lodged securely in the jail in the court house basement and set about getting a confession out of him. A search of his room had netted a pair of shoes with stains that might be blood, a few negligible things. The trial of Woo Dak San, alias Woo Foo, for the murder of Yee Foo, was set for the fall term of court, in September.

On the docket Yee Fong was referred to as Y. N. Fong, a name he had adopted in deference to American ways. Yee was his family name; the Chinese, more logical than Occidentals, put the surname first. The Yee family of Phoenix was said to have engaged Herman Lewkowitz to assist District Attorney Forrest Fielder in the prosecution.

Meanwhile the County Clerk's office was being annoyed by the rattling of window bars in the jail below them. Woo Dak San was trying to get dope. Deputy John St. John was down there with him.

The Deputy tipped against the wall the chair he had brought. There was no chair in the cell, not even a cot. The prisoner sat on the floor or paced up and down, begging, crying for dope. His color was bad, his whole body shaking.

"Now, Woo Dak, whyn't you come clean with me? I know you killed old Fong. You might as well admit it . . . You know I can't give you dope; I ain't got any dope." His blue eyes were kind, his drawling southern accent low and pleasant. "Only a doctor can do that. You know that . . . Well, now, Woo Dak, why should I get you a doctor? You won't do nothing for me. I'm just asking you to tell me the truth. I can't get a doctor till you tell me the truth."

At last — what long last to those tortured nerves — Woo Dak said: "All right. I'll talk. You get the doctor. When he gives me a shot I'll talk."

Dr. Bosley, coming with his little black bag found the prisoner "nervous, complaining of feeling sick. He asked for morphine." Woo Dak had his arm bared and stuck through the bars. "But no," said Deputy St. John, "not until you tell us the truth." The Doctor said: "Make up your mind, I'm in a hurry."

"Nothing doing," said Woo Dak, rolling down his sleeve. "That doctor was going to double-cross me," he told the Deputy later. That was nine o'clock in the morning. By noon Woo Dak, or his tortured nerves, thought differently about it. The Doctor testified later: "He insisted upon having it before he talked, but desire for it overcame his will power and he decided to talk."

But Deputy St. John put off the confession scene until after five when the Grand Jury would have recessed and District Attorney Forrest Fielder could be present. He attended, just around the corner from Woo Dak's cell, where he could hear without being seen. Dr. Bosley administered a hypodermic needle of morphine, Woo Dak's nerves soon settled, and he was ready. First he got the Doctor's promise of more dope as he needed it.

So Woo Dak San confessed to the murder of Yee Fong. He was not alone, he said. He named his accomplice, a Chinese who was never apprehended nor indicted nor questioned. The two entered Yee Fong's store late, Woo said. "I hit him with the ax and the other fellow put the knife in him." His accomplice, Woo Dak said, took all the money, promising to divide later. But he went away. Woo Dak suggested that the police look for him. But the police had their criminal.

Deputy St. John at once wired the Yee family's attorney in Phoenix that the suspect had confessed. Next morning Mr. Lewkowitz was in Silver City. Woo Dak agreed to repeat his confession "upstairs." In the sheriff's office were Mr. Lewkowitz and a stenographer, the Deputy and the prisoner. Later Mr. Yee of Phoenix joined them.

Mr. Lewkowitz said: "Just tell me and this lady will mark it down so I'll have a memorandum. I don't make notes very well."

Woo Dak told his story again. Then he signed the stenographer's book where they told him to. Nothing was read to him. Nor was he told that what he said might be used against him. But Woo Dak, returned to his cell, continued to get regular doses of morphine. He would crush the tablets in a spoon of water, heat it with a match and swallow it. Bit by bit Dr. Bosley reduced the quantity until one day Woo Dak complained: "This chalky damn stuff ain't got no kick; I'm going to quit."

One day Deputy St. John found a card hanging to Woo Dak's cell.

"Woo Dak San in jail for killing an old
Chinaman. Killed him with a hatchet.
Drove a knife through his head and
stole his money."

The deputies would find themselves troubled with other examples of Woo Dak's wry humor. Maybe it was Chinese face-saving. Once, asked if he was frightened Woo Dak answered: "I am a man."

Only one friend called on Woo Dak in jail: an old man who spoke with him in Chinese. The deputies, curious, persuaded another Chinese to listen in from a neighboring cell. The eavesdropper said he heard Woo Dak ask that his brother in Los Angeles be notified. He quoted: "Tell him to have my tong come over here and kill every Chinaman in Silver City." People began to whisper about "a tong killing."

Tongs, as few people know, are made in America, not in China. They were founded in California's wild early years when peace loving Chinese banded together against lawless whites. Tongs, like their contemporaries the vigilantes, occasionally used lawless methods; their dignified leaders had been known to hire "hatchetmen" for jobs unbecoming their own lofty correctness. Woo Dak hinted that he might have been a hatchetman. But latterly tongs were benevolent and protective lodges; the last "war" had been in San Francisco in 1921. Woo Dak said he had let his membership lapse. "I haven't paid dues for a long time; maybe they threw me out." It was pretty vague, but Silver City citizens planned to take in the trial, pleasantly apprehensive of a home town tong war.

160

On September 20, 1925, Woo Dak San, alias Woo Foo, was put upon his trial for the murder of Y. N. Fong, also known as Yee Fong. Raymond Richard Ryan was the judge. The jury included no Chinese. As the defendant stated that he had no money to employ counsel, the Court appointed Alvan N. White. Mr. Lewkowitz of Phoenix conducted the prosecution.

Judge Ryan was young, well-trained, and rigidly correct; but with a puckish Irish wit and a quick Irish temper sometimes hard to restrain. Mr. White was a splendid figure of a man, over six feet tall, weighing about two hundred and fifty pounds, with black hair and mustache, and black eyes. A Tennessean, he had not been long enough in the arid West to lose either his southern accent or his gift for rolling out forensic eloquence. A former superintendent of schools, he was forever ready to do his best for any one who seemed to him put-upon. Throughout the legal battles over Woo Dak San, Alvan White missed no chance to object, take exception, demur, appeal, or seek relief. Many people had driven miles to hear Mr. White; he was as surely an advocate for the defense as was ever Clarence Darrow. Mr. Lewkowitz was a firm believer in hanging the guilty. He believed Woo Dak San was guilty.

Woo Dak San, asked whether he pleaded guilty or not guilty, requested a private word with the Court. Judge Ryan leaned across the bench. The prisoner spoke low, with intensity. "Judge, that money they took away from me. That lotta money in China. I got mother there, wife and daughter. You promise send that money to China and I'll let 'em hang me!" The Judge, incensed at the suggestion of a private deal, brought his gavel down hard. "Not guilty," he ordered.

The whole story was told and retold with only omissions as

seemed expedient or inclusions denied to the jury — after the jury
had heard.

Doctor Bosley testified that he first saw Yee Fong's body after
it had been "prepared" by the undertaker, but that the ax wounds
in the head had certainly caused death. He said he had given Woo
morphine in the jail; that his mentality was all right at the time.
"Did you make any threats?" "No, sir." "Any offer?" "Yes, if he
would tell the truth regarding this alleged crime I would give him
morphine to relieve his condition."

Woo Dak, asked "Why did you make that confession?"
answered, "I made it for dope." "Did you know Mr. Lewkowitz
might use it against you?" "No." And again, "I was afraid they
wouldn't give me any if I didn't say anything. I had to say something." "Did you have a lawyer before that time?" "No." "Why
not?" "They would not let me have one."

Much of this was while the jury was out of the room, but the
Court admitted the confession. Mr. White was taking exceptions
all along.

Mr. St. John described the card Woo Dak had hung on his cell
door, saying that Mr. White had him remove it. Mr. White,
incensed, took the stand himself to maintain he had never seen it.
Woo Dak had a quiet cool smile. The jury was told to disregard
that evidence, but had heard it.

The Chinese who had been hidden to overhear Woo Dak's talks
with his caller, told how he had asked his tong to kill every Chinaman in Silver City. Woo Dak denied this.

Several Chinese testified that Woo Dak must have been broke;
that he had borrowed small sums: five, six, even one dollar when
he needed a haircut. Woo Dak said all these small items were pay-

ments on gambling debts; that he had no need to borrow; he was even thinking of buying and reopening the American Kitchen. An attorney confirmed this. He had drawn up preliminary papers, but the deal fell through. As to the money found on him, Woo Dak said he had earned it; some in Silver City, some before he came there. He had kept it wrapped in paper behind the stove in the American Kitchen.

Mr. Lewkowitz, for the prosecution, averred that guilt had been established beyond any reasonable doubt. He demanded the death penalty. Mr. White, convinced of his client's innocence and ready with both fact and authority, emphasized that all the evidence was circumstantial, that no motive had been shown, nor had it been proved that the money found on Woo Dak San had belonged to Yee Fong. The police had made no effort to apprehend another Chinese who had left town. The confession had been obtained under duress by torture of the most exquisite kind, and in an entirely illegal manner. The prisoner had not been warned that what he said would be used against him, nor had he been given a chance to read what the stenographer had written before he signed it. On this point Mr. White's well known eloquence rose to its height. His vibrant musical voice could be heard a block away, his gestures were compelling, his flashing eyes commanding. A stranger who had dropped in said: "I've just heard a $1,500 speech for nothing."

Judge Ryan, in his charge to the jury, justified his reputation for judicial fairness by making a special point of Woo Dak San's confession. He instructed the jury that before they could consider such a confession they must believe beyond a reasonable doubt that defendant had made it and that he made it "freely and without any exterior force, threats, or coercion, or any exterior influence that operated to deprive it of freedom, and made it when he was not under the influence of drugs." He reminded them that "the defendant was only a moderate user of the drug and was not in a condition so that he would admit away his life to obtain the small amount of the drug to relieve him." Though the Doctor promised Woo Dak San the drug if he told the truth, he had not promised him "immunity from the consequences of his crime"; nothing, that is, "to cause an innocent man to confess falsely."

The jury retired.

Everybody thought it was an open and shut case. A hop head Chinaman had murdered another Chinaman for his money. Might even have been a tong killing. Even Mr. White's eloquence had not won sympathy for his client who was, after all, considered a newcomer to Silver City. Still there was interest in hearing the verdict and when the rumor ran that the jury was returning, the court room filled again. The two deputies brought in their prisoner. A bailiff went for the jury.

Then a bird flew in out of the night. Afterwards people remembered differently. A sparrow, a dove, even a bat. Nobody thought of a Chinese nightingale with "bright-bronze breast and bronze-brown wing." It was a winged creature; dazzled by the light, it dashed against a window pane, could not find its way out. Women cupped their hands over their hair. The Judge ordered officers to put out the lights. The deputies closed in, hands on their prisoner. They heard a strange sound. Woo Dak San was giggling, his low breathless giggle.

"What have you got to laugh about?" asked Charlie Morrill. "You're going to be hanged for murder."

"No, they'll never hang me. You see that bird? That means I'm safe . . . Long ago a Chinese fortune teller told me. I'd be in much danger, she said, but a bird would save me. I don't believe those things, but you'll see."

The jury returned.

"Have you reached a decision?"

"No, Your Honor. We stand five to seven for conviction, but as one juror does not believe in capital punishment an agreement is impossible."

"What?" thundered the Judge. "What juror? . . . Stand up! Didn't you answer here that you had no scruples against the infliction of the death penalty?"

The juror in question was of Spanish extraction, spoke with a Spanish accent. "I can't," he said, "vote to have a man hanged."

The Judge, quick and choleric, ordered the Sheriff to hale the recalcitrant juryman off to jail. "Sixty days for contempt of court!" Judge Ryan, in his rage forgetting his correctness, had "busted the jury" instead of dismissing it.

Later the other jurymen petitioned for their colleague's relief, explaining that they were sure the man did not know English well enough to understand the question about capital punishment. Relief was granted. But the trial was lost. Woo Dak San could only be remanded to custody of the Sheriff and held for a new trial at the next term of court in March of 1926.

During that winter Woo Dak San got into trouble. Twice the deputies discovered that somebody had been trying to dig heavy stones out of the cell wall. Woo Dak said his cell mates were to blame; he was merely trying to put the plaster back when they caught him with trowel and wet plaster. Solitary on bread and water.

The second trial, in March, was like the first in testimony and in result. The second jury found Woo Dak San guilty of killing Yee Fong with an ax and pinning his head to the floor with a butcher knife. Judge Ryan sentenced him to be hanged by the neck until he was dead, dead, dead. "And the Lord have mercy on your soul." That was March 6, 1926.

Mr. White appealed the case on the ground that this second trial had placed his client in double jeopardy. Woo Dak San was now taken to the state penitentiary in Santa Fe where he soon made himself known as "a bad, bad Chinaman!" His record is a long list of infractions ranging from talking and laughing to threatening to kill another prisoner. Often he was deprived of privileges or put in solitary on bread and water. Some of his misdeeds showed originality and resourcefulness. As a professional cook, Woo Dak was put to work in the kitchen. One day, the Superintendent, tipped off by an informer, found jars of fermenting mash sizzling odorously in a warm spot behind the bake ovens. Woo Dak had been collecting potato peelings, left-over rice, occasional dried fruits, and sugar as available and was brewing up a bad-tasting but potent liquor. In all such cases he took his punishment stoically. Perhaps he was sustained by faith. He never mentioned a bird; maybe his trust was in his attorney.

Mr. White, unfaltering in his belief in his client's innocence, missed no opportunity to secure advantage for him. In 1929 the New Mexico Legislature passed a law making electrocution, instead of hanging, the penalty for murder. As a matter of form, they repealed the law providing hanging. Mr. White now came before the State Supreme Court with a long plea. Stated in non-legal language, he argued that as New Mexico had repealed its law making hanging the death penalty his client could not be hanged. Nor could he be electrocuted because that would be subjecting him to an *ex post facto* law. Moreover if the Supreme Court should so order, that body would be sentencing him to death, and the law makes that the duty of the District Judge. To make his case water-tight, Mr. White reminded the Honorable Justices of the irregular dismissal of the jury in the first trial. "The trial judge," he said, "in his hasty action of dismissal failed to hear or note defendant's objection to the discharge of the jury." Mr. White, missing nothing, also pointed out that the death sentence named "Warden" of the penitentiary, whereas "Superintendent" was the correct term. For all these reasons Mr. White pleaded that his client should be "either executed according to the law in force at the time of the crime, or discharged absolutely." The learned Justices had been handed a poser.

Woo Dak San, in his cell, must have thought of a bird darting about in a court room. It is not recorded that he mentioned it.

In June, and again in August, 1930, the Supreme Court handed down its decisions. It sustained the lower court in admitting Woo Dak San's confession for the reasons Judge Ryan had given in his charge to the jury. It found that the accused had not been placed in double jeopardy because the court had dismissed the jury before a verdict existed. It dismissed Mr. White's lesser complaints with a comment on his zeal in his client's behalf, and it ordered Woo Dak San back to Silver City to be sentenced to death in the electric chair.

Before this news had reached Woo Dak San in the penitentiary, science offered him a chance at escape. Hideyo Noguchi, the Japanese scientist, thought he had isolated the trachoma bacillus in an Albuquerque laboratory. For positive proof he needed a pair of human eyes to experiment with, preferably Asiatic. Dr. Francis Proctor, Dr. Noguchi's colleague in Santa Fe, suggested that Woo Dak San be offered a commutation of sentence if he would volunteer his eyes for the experiment.

"Will it make me blind?" asked Woo Dak. The doctors said they thought they could cure the disease after giving it to him; but they explained fully the chance he would be taking.

"I don't want to go blind," said Woo Dak, "but if they don't make me blind they can do it . . . I don't want any more court action."

Woo Dak San was now in the international news. Letters of approval and disapproval came from all the continents as well as all the states. Some offered to substitute for the Chinese; others threatened war on New Mexico if it allowed his sacrifice. As the protests outweighed the praise Dr. Proctor, who had hoped to serve science and help Woo Dak at once, withdrew his offer. So Woo Dak San, apprised of the Supreme Court's final ruling, was taken to Silver City where he was sentenced to the electric chair.

On the return, Deputy Charles Morrill served again as guard on what seemed Woo Dak's last journey. Again the deputy found his prisoner entertaining, if a bit baffling in his humor. Once, as they drove along through a stiff March wind blowing sand, Woo Dak shivered. "I'm cold," he complained. Then he giggled: "But when they get me on that hot seat I'll be warm enough. I'd better enjoy this cool while I can."

Thus Woo Dak San came back for his final winter in the penitentiary. Or was it to be final? Nobody had exorcised the mystic power of the bird. Nor had anything changed Mr. White's belief or determination. He now began trying to secure a pardon or a commutation of sentence. Woo Dak San's tong had not taken action, but his family in California and Arizona had been raising money; Mr. White, who had served so long and loyally as a court appointee, was to receive remuneration for his continuing efforts.

On March 17, 1932, the Governor issued an executive order commuting Woo Dak San's death sentence to life imprisonment. It seemed that the Chinese fortune teller's prophecy had been fulfilled; he would not be executed. He would drag out a life of dull obscurity in the penitentiary with only the variety provided by his unique misdeeds.

In time, Woo Dak's talent as a cook had won him a job in the Superintendent's family. During his hours of duty in that pleasant house he was still inside the walls but he had access to the telephone. Naturally guests came and went, taxis excited no comment. But one day a Santa Fe taximan was apprehended bringing contraband in to Woo Dak San in the Superintendent's kitchen. The load included not only an ample supply of liquor, but a requisitioned blonde. The culprit, after suitable discipline, was returned to the prisoners' kitchen.

Woo Dak San's family, unaware perhaps of the mitigations he was providing for himself, addressed a letter to the Secretary of the Board of Pardons in September, 1932. It begged Woo Dak San's release. "Another committed the crime, which is known to so many of us, his countrymen. He has spent seven years of torture — awaiting . . . the end, that of the rope or the chair. This form of punishment is more terrible than just plain imprisonment as you

169

will agree I am sure." It promised to see that Woo Dak San, if released, would leave New Mexico and be guaranteed work. The letter ends most politically. "Christmas time is near as also is the election period and I hope that your good party is returned to power in New Mexico."

The bird, or whatever providence presided over the destiny of Woo Dak San, had not ended its hovering care. In 1940 another governor, persuaded that there did remain a reasonable doubt of Woo Dak's guilt, granted him a full pardon. After serving fourteen years, Woo Dak San left New Mexico for good. It is said that he is living in Arizona. Wherever he is, whatever his educated beliefs, we must hope that he is burning joss sticks to the bird that darted into the court room to bring him assurance that he would never hang.

If that bird was a Chinese nightingale it must still be singing "One thing I remember; spring came on forever, spring came on forever."

9. New Mexico Tries Its Own

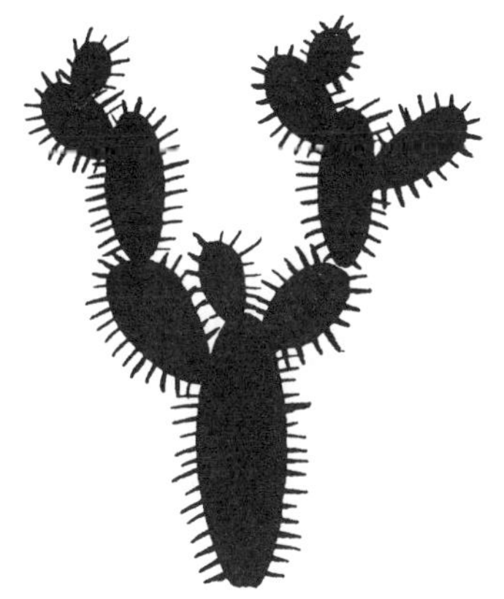

Victor Campos lived in Chihuahuita. He was a coal miner out of a job, a Mexican who had never bothered to take out naturalization papers. Victor did not think about such things. He had come from Mexico because he heard there were jobs with the Gallup American Coal Company. He had not learned English yet; he had been too busy, working in the mine and building himself a house. He had made his own adobes and bought what else he needed: door and window frames, locks and nails. He had signed a lease for the company land, but as he could not read he did not know that it contained a clause permitting the company to evict without notice. He thought he owned the house he had built and paid for. So did all Victor's neighbors and friends living in Chihuahuita.

As long as times were good Victor got along all right. He did not need English because his neighbors and fellow miners spoke Spanish. Even in church and at the meetings of his local of the National Miners Union, he heard only Spanish. In 1933 times were bad and Victor, with hundreds of other Gallup miners, went out on strike. It was an exciting time. The Governor ordered out the National Guard, and hundreds of men, including guards hired by the mine managers, were deputized. For six months martial law prevailed in Gallup. The miners won most of their demands and through their unemployed councils succeeded in making New Mexico's relief standards the highest in the country. But Victor and some of his friends noticed that men who had been most active in all this were not rehired when the mines reopened; they even had difficulty in getting federal relief.

The political situation in Gallup affected Victor Campos and his friends, though they were aliens with no vote. For years the Sheriff of McKinley County had been one of the Roberts: big-nosed, hard-fisted Bob or his younger brother, Dee. They agreed that enough force would solve all difficulties. But in 1935, M. R. Carmichael, a former mine guard, was sheriff with both the Roberts as deputies. Naturally, mine managers felt friendly toward peace officers who had been their hired guards; and business men in general, beholden to the mines for their incomes, friendly too. A gentleman whom all these law-and-order supporters counted on was William J. Bickel, Justice of the Peace. To certain irreverent lawyers, Mr. Bickel was known as "Bail-less" Bickel; occasionally he neglected to enter the amount of bail on his order to commit, forgetting the constitutional provision that a citizen may be imprisoned without bail only for murder or high treason.

172

Such was the situation in Gallup in the spring of 1935. Advertising had begun for the Inter-tribal Indian Ceremonial. Business was brisk with tourists spinning along Highway 66. Miners were getting a little work, a little relief. They held occasional meetings in the Spanish American Hall, but nobody paid much attention to them; and Navajos had no difficulty in getting liquor in spite of the federal laws.

Officers of the Gallup American Coal Company noticed that a good many men, not employed by and alleged to be blacklisted by the company, were living on company property. Probably with no connection, Clarence Vogel, a state senator, wanted just then to buy a tract of barren land near Gallup. What Mr. Vogel paid for or meant to do with those rocky hills is not of record. It is recorded that Mr. Vogel had been convicted of protecting the prostitution racket in Gallup. Anyway, Mr. Vogel acquired title to the land known as Chihuahuita; and, as owner, brought suit to evict the squatters there.

Judge Bickel appointed a constable who went over to Chihuahuita, armed with an order of possession, and nailed up the door of Victor Campos' house. It was a completely legal procedure. The constable was courteous, and even kindly set the Campos' furniture outside: a bed with sagging springs, an armchair that favored one shortened leg, a cook-stove, an empty cupboard.

While this legal business went on, the streets filled with people and intense excitement in several languages. If this happened to Campos it might happen to anyone. There were seventy-five or a hundred houses on Vogel's land; probably three hundred people lived there. Men remembered how hard it had been to pay for lumber and nails to build with. Women clutched their children

173

and wondered what it would be like on a cold night with no house and no place to go.

Three people took action. Eziquio Navarro, a short swarthy Mexican known to the police as a trouble-maker — that is, an active union man. Mrs. Lugardita Lovato, oldish and fat, but fiery. And Victor Campos, the dispossessed. They broke open the flimsy door and set the furniture back inside. All three were promptly arrested. Mrs. Lovato was released on her own recognizance, but the two men were taken to jail pending trial. "Bail-less" Bickel, living up to his pseudonym, failed to endorse the amount of bail on the warrant.

One can imagine how Chihuahuita reverberated with talk, but only one conversation has been reported. Leandro Velarde, it was later testified, had uttered revolutionary threats. Leandro was a big-bellied, cross-eyed Mexican given to a sort of moronic clowning. He was heard to say that he had a grudge against Sheriff Carmichael, and that officer against him; that he had a big belly and was ready to stick it out for the poor. He also said, "Let the officers take their guns; all we need is toothpicks." In court they tried to interpret *pica diente* as ice-pick, but without success. Still, some kind of pick had been mentioned, and poor Leandro with his wandering eye and childish boasting was to suffer for it.

On Sunday afternoon, April 3, there was a meeting of the unemployed in Spanish American Hall. Its regular business attended to, there was naturally talk about the Campos eviction. Leandro Velarde was there, still looking away with that unruly eye, still ready, presumably, to stick out his belly for the poor. No incendiary remarks were reported. Manuel Avitia was also present, a Mexican from

Durango who spoke no English. He was squat with strong muscles and darting hazel eyes in a ruddy pock-marked face. He had not been hired by the mines since he had discovered that the scales for weighing coal trucks marked the same weight after a dozen men clambered aboard. They found the control wires, but their complaints got them only a charge of tampering with the scales and black marks in the company's books. But Manuel had managed to get work most of the time as wood-cutter, barber, or motor mechanic.

Juan Ochoa was chairman of the meeting. A slim, quiet fellow with a face strained with sadness, a United States citizen born in New Mexico, he was equally at home in English or Spanish. He conducted an orderly meeting and appointed a committee to call on the Sheriff and ask if they might provide bail and counsel for Navarro and Campos. All quite according to the best American plan.

Sheriff Carmichael would not allow the committee to see his prisoners; it was supper time when no visitors were admitted. But he told them that the case would be heard by Justice Bickel at nine o'clock next morning and that they might attend the trial.

Monday, April 4, Sheriff Carmichael took his prisoners to Judge Bickel's office under guard of three armed deputies. Dee Roberts said later that they feared trouble. But Coal Avenue was quiet with few people in sight. Half an hour later, when the Judge had heard the case of a Navajo, two federal officers with the Indian passed without difficulty through a crowd around the door.

The gathering crowd was estimated at from fifty to two hundred and fifty: men, women and children, strikers, well-wishers, the curious, the belligerent. Judge Bickel's door was closed against them, though the law says something about speedy *and public* trial. Present were only Mr. Vogel, his attorney, the defendants, and police officers.

Navarro asked for time to procure counsel, which was granted at once and the case postponed until the next day.

If one peace officer had opened the door and explained that postponement, how surely tragedy could have been averted! Instead, Sheriff Carmichael stationed four officers inside the plate glass window on Coal Avenue to hide his next maneuver; he had decided to take his prisoners out by the back door and down the alley to the jail a block away. That show of secrecy raised the worry outside to frenzy. What was happening? Prosecution witnesses said the people cursed and pounded the glass; defense, that curious youngsters in front were pushed against it. Anyhow the window was broken. And, over that screen of solid backs, Navarro was seen to raise his arm. A gesture lends itself to divers interpretations. Was he waving goodbye and all right? Or was he beckoning the crowd around into the alley?

Somebody up the street yelled, "They're taking him out by the alley," and the crowd surged up Coal Avenue and around the corner into Third Street. The fateful alley leads from Third Street to Second where the jail stands, and onto it opens the back door of Mr. Bickel's office.

Deputy Fred Montoya, former mine guard, opened that door in time to see the crowd surge in with Leandro and Ignacio Velarde in front. Others testified that Solomon Esquivel was leading too. Leandro Velarde, always loud-mouthed, shook his fist and shouted, "Now you'll see it, *desgraciado!*" That means unlucky in the dictionary, but is a fighting word actually.

Solomon reached inside his coat, as though for a weapon, and yelled, "You move back! Leave them to us alone!"

Deputy Montoya judged it wise to retire, and did.

Sheriff Carmichael and Dee Roberts, undeterred, stepped out with Navarro struggling between them. Hoy Boggess and E. L. "Bobcat" Wilson followed with Campos.

Somebody shouted, "We want Navarro!"

Dee Roberts saw Juan Ochoa threatening him with a claw hammer. Boggess saw somebody grab for his prisoner, and he hurled a tear gas bomb into the rushing crowd, then estimated as seventy-five people. Boggess was knocked unconscious and his pistol disappeared underfoot. But his bomb went off. At the same instant a shot was fired, apparently by Ignacio Velarde standing across the alley. Roberts saw Sheriff Carmichael turn, blood spurting from his face. He eased his chief down to the pavement, drew his gun and shot Velarde and then Solomon Esquivel, who fell and began to get up, so Roberts shot him again. Roberts testified later that he saw four or five men on top of Boggess, kicking and pommeling him—Ochoa and Manuel Avitia among them. Boggess had got to his feet. Deputy Wilson cried, "I'm shot!" Boggess grabbed Wilson's gun and he and Roberts fired at the running people. Twelve or fifteen shots were heard altogether. The blowing tear gas was blinding everybody, but these things were seen by two women on a roof.

Meanwhile, Sherman Porter, a mine guard passing on Coal Avenue, saw Manuel Avitia run out of the alley with a pistol. Kelsey Pressly also saw Avitia with something "that looked like a gun," but when arrested Avitia had no gun. Mr. Pressly had also captured a pick handle on a thong from a man he afterward identified as Agustin Calvillo.

By that time, Navarro and Campos had disappeared, and Sheriff Carmichael lay dead. One bullet had struck him in the face and passed out through the neck. This bullet was never found. The other entered under the left arm and lodged in the left shoulder. Either shot might have been fatal. He died instantly. His own gun had not been fired. Boggess' gun was never found, nor were those of Ignacio Velarde, whom Dee Roberts had killed, nor Solomon Esquivel, who died later from his wounds.

Bob Roberts, who had seen the fracas from the jail window, reached his brother in time to identify nine people. He and Dee ordered the people away, sent Bobcat Wilson to a hospital where they probed a bullet out of him. Hoy Boggess was groggy from that crack on the head, but he soon recovered.

At once Dee Roberts, sheriff now, began a clean-up. John Doe warrants were sworn out and dozens of stalwarts were deputized and sent through Chihuahuita. Ostensibly seeking the missing guns, they also turned up Communist and union literature, and evidence that certain people were not American citizens. The searchers were accused of threatening women, annoying young girls, frightening children. They arrested several hundred people whom they crowded into the city and county jails; even the court rooms were filled. Sixteen women and four children spent a stifling night in two small cells. Citizens of Gallup walked in fear, for the affair was already being called a riot, and the people concerned, a mob.

On April 6, a dapper young man stepped off the train from Los Angeles and announced himself as attorney for the Civil Liberties Union sent to see that justice was done. A. L. Wirin, veteran of many labor rows, was aggressive, Jewish, and an outsider; none of these characteristics endeared him to the solid citizenry of Gallup, to say nothing of the officers who had seen their chief shot down. Somebody told Mr. Wirin to be on his way, and he went on to

178

Santa Fe to seek support. There he found many people stirred by the flagrant injustice of arresting a couple of hundred men, women, and children for the murder of a man killed by two shots; by the illegal search; and because no counsel had been provided for the defendants, most of whom spoke no English, and all of whom were poor.

In their behalf the Gallup Defense Committee was organized with fifteen original members. Judge Miguel A. Otero, sitting in the case, appointed Wheaton Augur of Santa Fe to assist in the defense. Mr. Clarence Lynch of the International Labor Defense also joined the defense counsel.

The Gallup imbroglio had now swelled up into a major engagement in the CLASS WAR. Mr. Wirin was quoted as calling it "the greatest civil liberties and labor case now before the country." The radical and liberal press made comparisons with the Scottsboro boys, Mooney, and Sacco and Vanzetti. Letters, telegrams, and printed postal cards poured in on the judge, demanding the immediate release of the Gallup workers. Little words like "request" and "please" did not appear in their stern lexicon, nor phrases to imply that any New Mexico public servant could be fair. This was poor psychology. Perhaps nobody was trying to get anybody's dander up; but the miners' fervid friends, with their talk of class war and martyred miners, certainly stirred up fears of a Communist uprising.

Luckily for the defendants, Gallup lay in the jurisdiction of Judge Otero, a consistent liberal. Most notable contemporary member of a famous old family, Judge Otero is short and fair with such a fresh young face that his fuzzy pate suggests hair not yet arrived rather than retreating. Well-schooled and unruffled by extravagances from either side, he injected the first note of common sense into the situation.

In Gallup Carl Howe, a Communist organizer but not an attorney, had appeared for the miners and waived preliminary hearing for them, thereby causing them to be bound over for trial without bond. Mr. Wirin and Mr. Lynch called upon Judge Otero in Santa Fe and demanded immediate hearing. Judge Otero acceded without demur, and had the accused lodged in the penitentiary to await the preliminary hearing.

The first fury having somewhat abated, instead of a hundred and fifty, fifty-two men and women were held for the hearing. Several of the accused had not been in Gallup on the day of the riot, and three of the wounded were too ill to appear. So forty-five marched into the court room, two-by-two with folded arms, ragged, pitiful. Most of them spoke no English — one, a Slav, had neither Spanish nor English, and was dismissed. They were all accused of killing Sheriff Carmichael and conspiring to aid a prisoner to escape.

The hearing opened before a distinguished audience. Santa Fe's art and literary colonies attended in force; and Judge Otero invited members of the Gallup Defense Committee to sit inside the rail — to the extreme exasperation of the State's attorneys whose sanctum was profaned by "long-haired men and short-haired women." As a concession to conservatives' fears, a policeman frisked all comers at the door. He discovered one gun and had its owner on his way to the hoosegow when Judge Otero recognized him as a milkman who had a permit to carry a pistol.

On the third day arrived David Levinson to represent the International Labor Defense Association. A small, keen-faced Philadelphia lawyer with formal attire and pince-nez on a long black ribbon, he added great tone to the proceedings. Things now moved fast. Three more defendants were dismissed, but were promptly rearrested by US Immigration officers. Mr. Levinson, enraged, lost his urbane calm and snatched at an officer's arm. Cries, then: "He's interfering with a federal officer!" But Judge Otero, quick too, had already left the court room and was under no compulsion to charge the lawyer with contempt of court. Nothing came of the episode except the charge that the State had got rid of several important alibi witnesses. Demands went to Madam Secretary Perkins in Washington.

Mr. Wirin demanded that his clients be allowed to walk with their arms down instead of folded in the manner of convicts. Granted.

When the evidence was in, Mr. Wirin made a fiery plea to "let these people go back to their miserable shacks, their back-breaking work in the coal mines, to relief or starvation or whatever their lot in life." Mr. Augur also spoke, contending that the evidence of the Gallup officers was prejudiced.

Judge Otero held ten men for the murder of Sheriff Carmichael and for aiding a prisoner to escape. Four he held without bail. Juan Ochoa, whom Dee Roberts had seen flourishing a claw hammer; Manuel Avitia, whom Sherman Porter had seen with a gun in his hand; Leandro Velarde, he of the "ice-pick"; and Agustin Calvillo, whom Chief of Police Pressly had disarmed of a club. The others he held on $7,500 bail each, which might as well have been a million as far as the indigent defendants were concerned. His Honor had the whole party taken back to Gallup in a State bus.

Many dispassionate observers had expected the Judge to dismiss all the defendants for insufficient evidence. Certainly there had been no proof that any one of these men had killed Sheriff Carmichael. But they had been in the crowd, and four of them were shown to be armed; the killing of an officer in the discharge of his duty is a serious offense. Under the New Mexico law, as well as the law invoked in the Haymarket case and upheld by the United States Supreme Court, all the members of a mob may be held as participants of a murder. And men may be held for trial "for probable cause, though conviction for a crime requires proof beyond a reasonable doubt."

Judge Otero, who had been saluted in the radical press as an honorable judge, lost face there, and was also distinctly out of favor with conservatives. Fears dominated both sides. In Gallup a mass meeting was forbidden, armed men were posted on every corner, and a firehose laid ready to quench any inflammable talk. One car full of tourists were stopped and frightened half out of their wits before they could prove their hundred-per-centness.

When David Levinson went to Gallup to gather evidence, he demanded police protection, and Earl Irish, a State Trooper, was delegated to accompany him. With them went Robert Minor, representative of the *Daily Worker,* and members of the Gallup Defense Committee.

They found Gallup's Harvey Hotel Navajo full of people whom they described as "stooges, rats, and spies." Even a group of women playing bridge looked to them suspicious. Fearful of dictaphones in their rooms and of eavesdroppers in the lobby, Mr. Levinson and Mr. Minor met Mrs. Julia Bartol, a union organizer, outdoors to discuss witnesses.

As they sat in Mrs. Bartol's car other automobiles drove up alongside. Masked men got out, guns were shown, the two men were beaten insensible, dragged into two cars and thrown on the floor. Minor called repeatedly, but though this happened in the center of Gallup nobody responded. Mrs. Bartol saw the cars cross the tracks and head north. She started to follow, but a masked youth standing near advised her not to, so she ran into the hotel, crying, "They've got them! They've taken them for a ride!"

The Gallup Defense Committee got on the long distance at once, calling Governor Tingley, Judge Otero, State's Attorney Patton, the *Albuquerque Journal.* Sheriff Roberts was out of town. The excited committee complained that deputies and other people in the lobby were elaborately uninterested. The Attorney General refused to move until he had word from the Gallup authorities. At three A.M. the Governor, disturbed by repeated phone calls, finally agreed to send additional troopers.

Sheriff Roberts arrived at eleven o'clock, but though Mrs. Bartol told him the cars had gone north, his patrols searched westward all that night.

At noon the next day, Governor Tingley was called on the telephone by Mr. Levinson, speaking from the Indian hospital at Tohatchi, about twenty-five miles from Gallup. He demanded police and military protection, and an immediate investigation. He said he and Mr. Minor were safe, though badly shaken and hurt.

The Levinson and Minor story, broadcast all over the country, was that they had driven for about an hour, were beaten anew whenever they regained consciousness, and finally dumped on the ground and kicked. Hoods had been pulled over their heads so they could not describe their abductors nor give the license numbers of the cars. They could only say that the men were well-dressed, the cars new and good.

When Mr. Levinson tried reasonably to explain his mission in Gallup, someone said roughly, "We don't want speeches."

When Minor asked for his fountain pen, he was told that he would not need it in hell.

Both men thought they would surely be lynched, but the final sentence was, "Get out of here and stay out . . . If you ever come back, we'll kill you." So they were left.

As soon as they were able the two attorneys shed the blood-soaked hoods and began to walk, leaving markers on fences, and about dawn they reached the hogan of Benny Tohe, a Navajo, who gave them food and coffee and took them on to Tohatchi.

Two theories developed immediately. The kidnaping was an outrageous violation of all civil rights, vigilantism at its worst. Or it was a fake show, staged to discredit the New Mexico authorities. The victims and their supporters telegraphed everybody from the President down, demanding military protection, congressional investigation, immediate punishment. Attorney General Patton promised to clear the matter up, whether it was real or a frameup. Earl Irish, a detective, several Navajos, an AP man, and members of the Gallup Defense Committee went over the ground and reported that the kidnaping was real. Sheriff Roberts thought "it looked mighty funny" and "might be a hoax."

An old resident commented on the affair:

"Well, if those birds didn't precisely kidnap themselves, they certainly laid themselves open to trouble. We don't care much for eastern dudes and their women telling us how bad we are. A few years ago, they'd have danced to a brace of pistols. As it was, all they got was a good scare, and it was probably coming to 'em."

Mr. McIntosh, Assistant District Attorney, went to interview the victims after their return to Gallup. Their injuries had been found superficial by Gallup physicians whom the *New Masses* called "petty political hirelings." But both men were utterly miserable, aching, and nerve-shocked when Mr. McIntosh came to demand the evidence they had: masks, a belt from a coat, such things.

Mr. Minor said, "This is another frameup."

"Yes," said McIntosh, "this kidnaping is a frameup."

Whereupon Minor said, "The kidnapers are safe in your hands."

And McIntosh, "You are a God damned liar."

So the defense could say that the District Attorney had refused decent investigation — undoubtedly true — and the District Attorney, that the victims had refused to deliver him their evidence — equally true. Nobody was ever brought to trial for this brutal attack.

On Saturday, May 5, after two days of recriminations, Judge Otero arrived in Gallup on another case. He was pursued into his room by the enraged Mr. McIntosh, demanding that Mr. Minor be forced to turn over his evidence. Mr. McIntosh stood ready, he said, with all the most scientific crime detection machinery to run down and find and prove. He had not rushed into the press with hysterical statements. He had kept his investigation on a high plane. Convinced that he could put his hand on the kidnapers if he had the evidence, he suggested that the victims did not want the malefactors caught.

Mr. Minor also sought the Judge with his complaint against Mr. McIntosh. He finally agreed to turn over his evidence to the Court. So the Judge, as he shaved and changed his shirt, dictated a statement to his court stenographer, and took over the evidence.

As Mr. Minor complained that the Governor had refused a guard, Judge Otero ordered Earl Irish to escort Mr. Levinson and

Mr. Minor to Santa Fe, and telephoned his own physician to ascertain the extent of their injuries. Both men, happily, were found not too seriously wounded to speak in public within a few days. The round-faced boyish Judge had again kept his balance and sense of humor.

Mr. Wirin, convinced that a jury of Gallup citizens would not sympathize with either miners or kidnap victims, demanded a change of venue. Judge Otero designated San Juan County on the Colorado line — a rich agricultural county of farmers speaking both English and Spanish, and with no labor troubles.

The prosecution now disqualified Judge Otero: a privilege which the New Mexico law permits to either side without showing cause. As the contesting parties could not agree on a substitute, the Supreme Court appointed Judge James McGhee of Chavez County. Judge McGhee appointed to defend the accused miners not untried boys, but two of the most distinguished lawyers in the state. Hugh Woodward had been United States District Attorney; John Simms a Justice of the State Supreme Court. No amount of money could have bought better counsel.

Mr. Levinson and Mr. Minor, back in New York, were received by twelve hundred vociferous Communists, with police escort, parades, and speeches to celebrate their safe return from the WAR. They did not appear again in the case.

The Gallup Defense Committee retained the firm of Donovan, Leisure, Newton, and Lombard of 2 Wall Street. These gentlemen asked for more time to prepare the case, but Judge Simms and Mr. Woodward agreed to appear in October, so the trial was set for October 3. The Wall Street firm, expected to overawe, sent two young men just out of law school who generously asked only their expenses. They flew out and flew back, put up at good hotels, and even attended the trial. Perhaps their eastern accent and their daily long distance talks with New York impressed the San Juan farmers enough to be worth the thousands they set the Gallup Defense Committee back.

The trial was held in Aztec, an elm-shaded town of big frame houses and gardens, more like New England than New Mexico. Harvest was ripe, and housewives overfed the lawyers with fried chicken, homemade preserves and pies. As this was a great battle in the Class War, San Juan County obliged; the shaky jail was reinforced by an eight-foot barbed wire fence and a bloodhound was chained to a tree. He at once made friends with the prisoners and bayed at them musically during the trial. A squad of State Troopers in striped trousers and Sam Browne belts added a strange note in New Mexico where officers are generally indistinguishable from anybody else. His Honor's pistol clearly bulged his coat tails, and he was constantly attended by Sam McCue, also thoroughly armed.

The first morning Earl Irish, bored with his role in the Class War, leaned against a window and knocked loose the sash which came down with a bang like a gunshot. His Honor on the bench, his bodyguard, the impanelled jurymen, the public, counsel, and prisoners leapt as one, while the guilty trooper sheepishly braced the window up again.

Every morning dodgers appeared in the streets. "SAVE THE GALLUP WORKERS. YOU MAY BE NEXT. UNITE." Jittery citizens, organized as the United American Patriots, reported that hundreds of Reds were coming from Gallup. Defense asked a recess. While Mr. McCue guarded His Honor in a close-shuttered room, Judge Simms and Mr. Woodward strolled in the plaza where they met a couple of kids with pea-shooters. "The invading Army!" said John Simms.

The Leftists, no less jittery, whispered that Mr. McCue had planted a machine gun behind the fern in a window facing the Court House. When the *Daily Worker* reporter was threatened with contempt proceedings, her paper reported that she had been jailed, and the Judge was deluged with telegrams demanding her release. Doubtless His Honor enjoyed replying that the lady sat as usual at the press table.

The New Mexico papers carried daily first page stories throughout the affair. The *New Masses* of October 22 reported: "The daily press carries no mention of the case. New Mexico exercises a strict censorship on what goes on at Aztec, a little town away from a railroad, dominated by vigilantes."

Despite all this, twelve good men and true were found who had heard or read nothing of the case, who belonged to no patriotic societies, and who were unprejudiced and uninfluenced. Before their virgin minds, the whole tale was unrolled again.

The State undertook to prove that Eziquio Navarro and Victor Campos, held for housebreaking, were aided to escape by a rioting mob, and that they or someone else killed Carmichael and wounded two other officers. They also charged conspiracy, which would make the whole mob responsible for whatever happened.

Witnesses testified that the crowd in front of Justice Bickel's office was "hollering and cursing" as it rushed around into the alley. Cross examination established that many of this crowd were women and children and so considerably reduced the effect of truculence.

188

Officers testified. Hoy Boggess told how he saw threatening gestures, how he threw his tear gas bomb, was struck unconscious and knew nothing more until he saw Bobcat Wilson coming toward him wounded and doubled up with pain. The State did not call Mr. Wilson, and Defense did not learn at once that he and Mr. Boggess had left town soon after that officer's testimony.

Several people had seen Ignacio Velarde shoot and fall, killed by Dee Roberts; and Solomon Esquivel fall wounded to rise and drop a second time, dead. That one of these men killed the sheriff seemed likely.

The State introduced a ballistics expert and pistols tenderly handled in velvet cases. The defense agreed to admit without argument that these were the guns in question. They established easily that the bullet which killed Sheriff Carmichael might have come from Hoy Boggess' gun! That was their only interest in armament, for no other guns had been found, even in that bullying search through Chihuahuita.

Sherman Porter testified that he had seen Manuel Avitia with a gun, but cross examination made it seem doubtful that as short a man as Manuél could have been seen from the corner in the midst of a hundred people. Nor was that pistol found.

The only other weapon produced was the club Mr. Pressly had taken from Agustin Calvillo, but how it had been used was not established.

To prove conspiracy, the State cited Leandro's talk about being ready to die for the poor; his grudge against Sheriff Carmichael; and his ice-pick — or was it toothpick? Two women testified they had seen Leandro, at home after the ruction, take an ice-pick from the bib of his overalls and put it in the icebox. So there was the pick again — *ice* this time, not *tooth*. State's Attorney Chavez tried to make the witnesses name an ice-pick in connection with the earlier threats, but they stuck to the lighter article.

Dee Roberts was the State's star witness — the intrepid officer who had seen his chief and friend fall dead at his side, and who had unhesitatingly shot and killed two malefactors. His most telling bit was that he saw Juan Ochoa coming at him with a claw hammer. Nobody else saw that. He also saw Ochoa and Avitia kicking and beating Hoy Boggess as he lay on the ground. And nobody else saw that. On cross examination Mr. Roberts admitted to arresting over a hundred people, many of whom he had never seen. He recognized only eight in the alley.

The two ladies, from their grandstand seat on the roof, had seen the crowd in Coal Avenue and then in the alley. They had seen Ignacio shoot and fall, Solomon fall, Hoy Boggess fall; they had been blinded with tear gas. One of them was led gently along in cross examination to describe a rioting mob armed with flails, pitchforks, and pruning hooks — more suitable, perhaps, for a Russian mob in the movies than a gang of miners in Gallup. The State rested.

The defense moved the dismissal of all charges, but was overruled. Judge Simms and Mr. Woodward then asked an adjournment for a few minutes' talk with their ten clients. Through an interpreter they stated their opinion that only four men need testify: Juan Ochoa, Leandro Velarde, Manuel Avitia, and Augustin Calvillo. There was enough testimony against them to require them to take the stand in their own defense. The attorneys did not believe that the State had produced enough evidence to convict the other six of any crime, but they explained the seriousness of the charges that might bring any of them to the electric chair. They asked these accused men to decide whether or not they wished to testify. Willie Gonzales, a high school graduate spoke for himself: "I will take our lawyers' advice. I will not go on the witness stand. Give me liberty or give me death!" The others followed Willie's lead.

Back in court, defense counsel introduced witnesses to reduce Leandro's "ice-pick" to "toothpick." Manuel Avitia, in his own defense, testified that walking on Coal Avenue he had heard firing and rushed into the alley. There he picked up a crying child and, stumbling over a gun, he picked that up to carry it to safety. As he went out of the alley, somebody took the gun from him. He admitted to being at the meeting in Spanish American Hall, but knew of no conspiracy and had not struck or kicked Hoy Boggess.

Juan Ochoa also testified. Three witnesses supported his statement that he had stood talking with them in Coal Avenue when they heard the firing in the alley.

On cross examination, Mr. Chavez asked Ochoa if he had organized the union, the unemployed council, and if he were a Communist. Immediate objections. Sustained.

Judge Simms and Mr. Woodward, knowing that a Communist had as much right to fair trial as a Republican, knew too that a Republican's chances were better. Aware of the humor of the situation and enjoying their license as court appointees, they were forever conscious of their responsibility to save ten men from the electric chair. So, in the brilliant defense, they showed that these men could not be proved to have conspired, to have fired a fatal shot, to have aided prisoners to escape. Even Avitia, seen with a gun, had not been seen to shoot it. Several people had seen Ignacio Velarde fire before he fell; and there was no proof that Sheriff Carmichael had not been killed by *one of his own officers.*

Mr. Woodward, for the defense, summed up the facts of the case and the law. Everyone was impressed by his serene face, his good humor, his complete reasonableness. His bald head, as will be seen, affected only one of his clients. Judge Simms spoke for each of the defendants, picturing helpless, poverty-stricken people caught in a wave of hate.

As his smooth, mellifluous voice flowed on, Sam McCue, Judge McGhee's bodyguard stood wringing his hands and muttering, "My God, I wish he'd hush! My God, I wish he'd hush!"

The jury brought in a verdict of acquittal for seven men, including Agustin Calvillo. The other three: Juan Ochoa, Manuel Avitia and Leandro Velarde were found guilty of murder in the second degree with a recommendation for clemency. Judge McGhee sentenced all three to from forty-five to sixty years at hard labor.

As His Honor pronounced sentence, Leandro Velarde, the knight of the toothpick, begged that in the penitentiary he would not be subjected to a haircut like Mr. Woodward's. Such close cropping, he feared, might endanger his errant eye.

Defense asked an appeal, which the court allowed. Judge McGhee, having restrained himself during the long trial, let go at last. He reminded the defendants that they had been defended by appointed counsel who had received none of the large sums raised for their defense. "So," he said, "somebody must have plenty of money to finance your appeal . . . I hope that the members of the Supreme Court will be spared the abuse, the threats, and attempted intimidation which has been practiced on me . . . and upon Judge Otero . . . The courts of the United States stand as a protection for the poor . . . We don't operate our courts in New Mexico and in the United States by mob rule . . . You prisoners have received as able defense as I have seen presented in any court . . ."

The Supreme Court, where Judge Simms and Mr. Woodward appeared without the support of the New York law firm, reversed the judgment in regard to Leandro Velarde. Juan Ochoa and Manuel Avitia served a short while and were pardoned at the recommendation of the Board of Pardons and Paroles. So the last of the ten accused regained their freedom. New Mexico had tried its own.

THE
PHOTOGRAPHS

Colonel Ethan W. Eaton, leader of
the Vigilantes of Socorro.

P. Stoddart Studio, Socorro

The little adobe Methodist chapel.

In 1875, one Alexander A. McSween appeared in Lincoln bringing his
young wife west in an oxcart. They became friends of Billy the Kid.

The Lincoln County Court House where
Billy the Scapegoat was jailed.

Barnes & Caplin, Albuquerque

Did Colonel Albert J. Fountain
disappear into the White Sands?

Their shifting, heavy waves keep
their secret well.

Black Jack was composed.

A Navajo trading post is a center of trade and gossip.

Milton Snow, Santa Fe

Barnes & Caplin, Albuquerque

In Taos "Old Man" Manby was
a familiar figure with his dog.

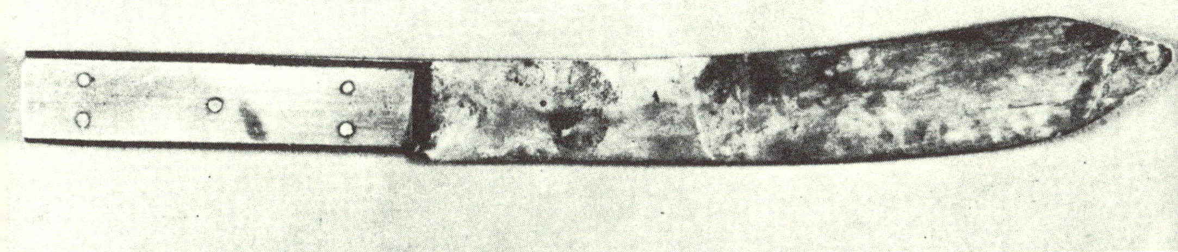

Was Woo Dak San the killer who used this knife?

His attorney, Alvan N. White,
thought he was not.

Deputy Sheriff St. John
thought he was.

 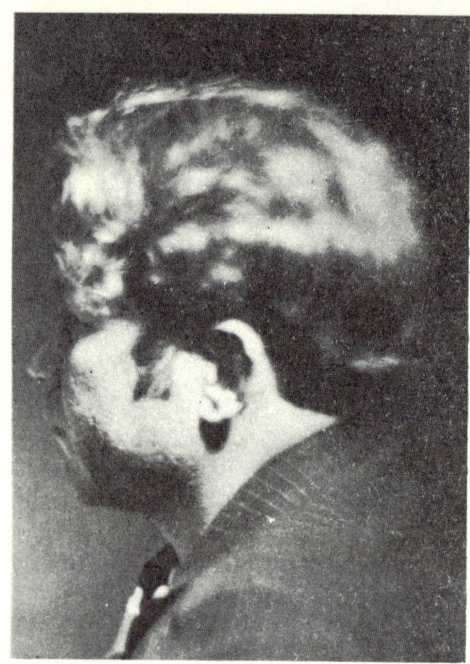

Manuel Avitia was a Mexican from Durango who spoke no English.

 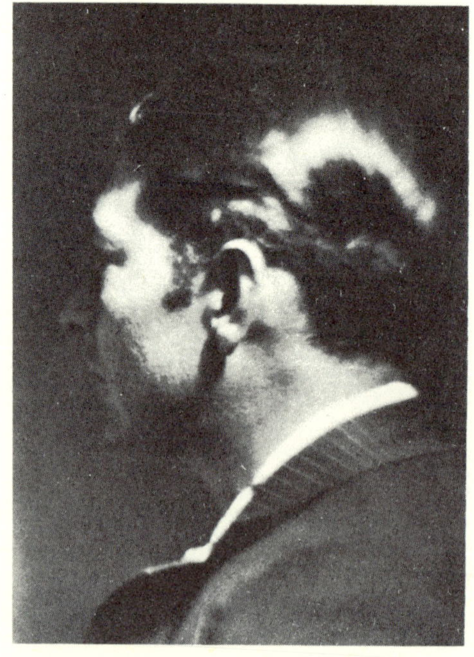

Juan Ochoa, with a face strained with sadness, was an American citizen equally at home in English or Spanish.